Nikon Z7 Illustrated Guide

A Visual Handbook to Z7 Mastery, from Beginner to Pro

By

Herbert Gunta

TABLE OF CONTENTS

INTRODUCTION

The Z7 introduces a comprehensive touchscreen technology which allows you to modify the majority of the camera's features and functionalities without the need for the Multi-selector. By touching the LCD monitor, you can choose menus and submenus related to the camera and make changes. Similar to how you would, on a smartphone, you can pinch and extend your fingers to zoom in and out of one picture and swipe to go to another one.

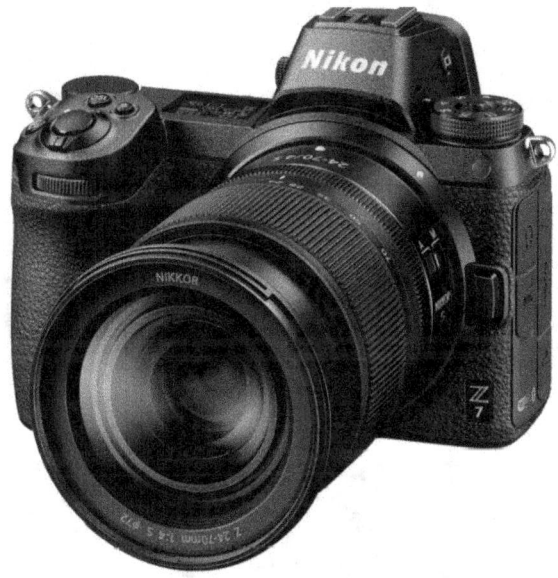

The Z7's electronic viewfinder (EVF) allows you to preview photos, modify the camera settings and menu settings, and review photos and movies. You can utilize the Z7's EVF for almost all camera operations and switch off the rear LCD panel if you choose to. You can also review a picture in the EVF before

5

taking it. You can quickly see the outcome of exposure and color balance changes as you make them without taking your eyes off the viewfinder.

For the most precise exposures, you can also use a live histogram in the EVF. The Z7's electronic viewfinder is so quick, accurate, and clear that you may not even realize you are using one.

Nikon's Z-mount lenses are compatible with the Z7, or you can use your preferred F-mount Nikkor lenses with the optional Nikon FTZ adapter. Nikon states that the FTZ adapter can be used to attach more than 350 different F-mount Nikkor lenses on the camera; this allows you to utilize a variety of current lenses.

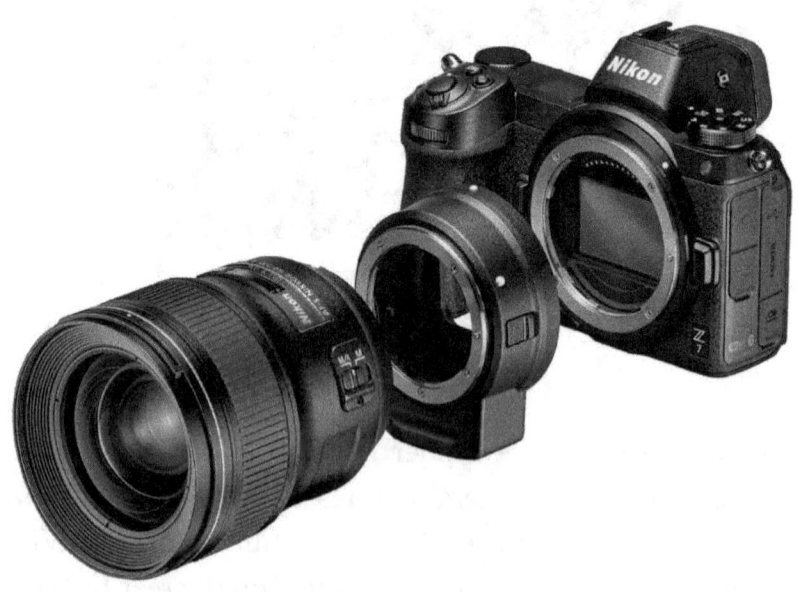

With Z-mount lenses, the camera has in-body 5-axis image stabilization; with the FTZ adapter, it offers in-body 3-axis image stabilization for F-mount lenses. All lenses placed on the camera or adapter feature VR (vibration reduction), including the older manual focus lenses, since the stabilization is integrated into the camera body. Imagine being able to handhold your older at slower shutter speeds (up to five stops) when they do not have VR. For those who like to handhold the camera, in-body virtual reality, also known as IBIS (in body image stabilization), really makes a difference.

Configuring the Camera for the First Time

Your Nikon Z7 can be quickly and easily set up for the first time once you have unpacked and checked your camera. All you really need to do is charge the battery, connect a lens, insert a memory card, and set the time. To properly set up your camera, however, if this is your first time using one, you need first learn how to utilize the menu button, command dials, and touch screen. These are covered in further details below;

Learning to Use the Command Dials and Multi Selector

During this first setup procedure, there are a few activities you must do, most of which utilize the MENU button, the multi/sub-selector buttons, and the pad.

1. MENU Button: This button hardly needs an explanation; just press it to bring up the menu options. Press it again to quit most menus or, in certain

situations, to confirm and exit your selected menu option.

2. This Multi-selector Pad: It is made up of a thumbpad-sized button with notches on it for left, right, up, and down, as well as diagonally. The multi selector: This is often used for navigating, such as switching between menus, advancing or reversing the display of an image series during picture review, and altering the kind of photo information that is shown on the screen. It can also be used to pick one of the user-selectable focus regions on the viewfinder and LCD monitor displays in place of the sub-selector "joystick".

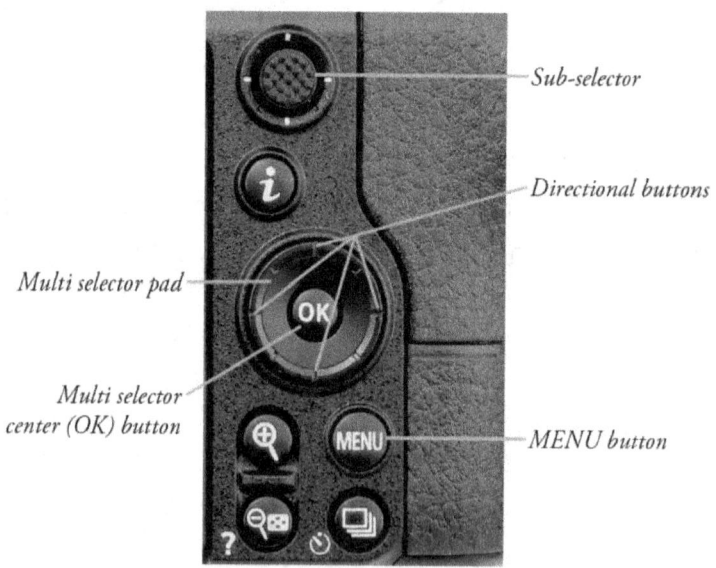

3. Multi Selector Center (OK) Button: To choose a highlighted item from a menu list, press the center button together with the right directional button.

Additionally, the middle button can be used as an Enter or OK key.

4. The Sub-selector Button: The sub-selector can be pressed down like a button or operated like a joystick. The sub-selector joystick's default navigational purpose is to select the focal point alone, which is a helpful control. Custom Setting f2: Custom Control Assignment allows you to implement actions such as menu navigation scrolling and playback using the joystick. By default, pressing the center button of the sub-selector locks focus or exposure (like an AE/AF lock button). However, Custom Setting f2 allows the button to be customized to do other functions.

5. The Main Command Dial and Sub-command Dial: The Z7's front and back include the main command dial and sub-command dial, respectively. While the subcommand dial modifies a secondary or alternative option, the main command dial is used to control parameters like shutter speed. For instance, in manual exposure mode, the shutter speed is adjusted with the main command dial while the aperture is adjusted with the sub-command dial. (In both scenarios, the exposure meter on the Z7 must be turned on for the dial to be "active" for these changes.) After a certain period, the meter will turn off automatically. To turn it back on and use the main and sub-command dials, you must touch the shutter release button to wake the camera.

Making Use of the Touch Screen

A multitude of touch functions are supported by the swiveling LCD display. It can be used, for instance, to adjust several settings or exit menus. However, while shooting in live view and playing back images, the touch screen can be really helpful. This is a list of actions you can take with the touch screen:

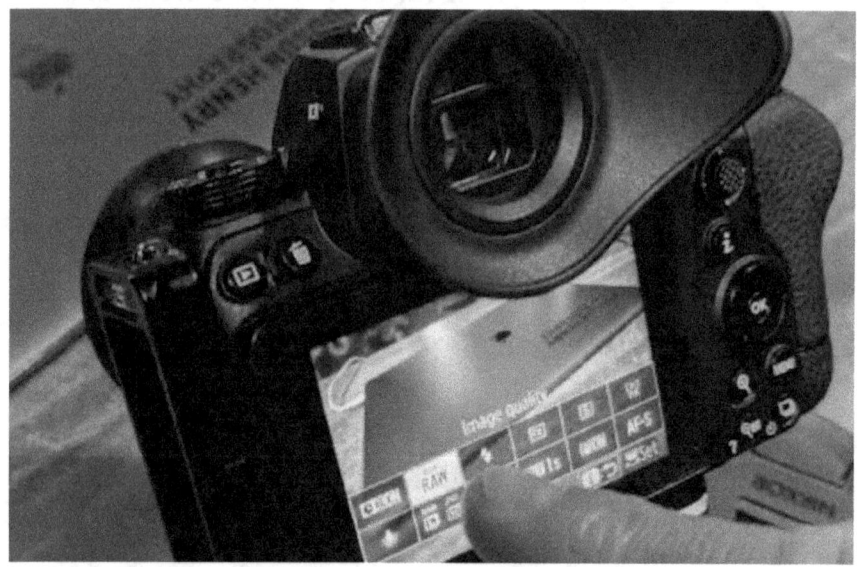

1. In Playback Mode:

- Navigate between images: To navigate between photographs as they are being played back, just flip the screen.

- Enlarge or reduce in size: Double-tapping the touch screen allows you to enlarge or reduce the size of a picture.

- Move the zoomed area: To move the zoomed area, slide your finger around the display.

- Watch movies and thumbnails: You can move between movies and index thumbnails.

2. In Photo Shooting Mode (with the LCD screen active):

- Take images: When the monitor is in photo mode, you can snap pictures by tapping the touch screen instead of pushing the shutter release. (However, tapping will not start a video capture.)

- Choose a focal point: You can tap a spot on the touch screen to designate a focus point in the Photo and Movie modes.

- Put text here: You can touch the on-screen keyboard to input text while using a text entry screen (for instance, to enter copyright information in the Setup menu). That is far quicker than the other option, which involves laboriously moving the spotlight from one character to another using the directional buttons.

In the Setup menu, you can also completely deactivate touch functionality or simply allow touch functionality for Playback features, which will prevent touch menu navigation. Using the Touch Controls item, you can additionally choose the direction for "flicks" in full-frame playback (left/right or right/left). Moreover, you can disable the Touch Shutter/AF function by touching an indicator that shows up on the left side of the screen whether filming a video or watching live. A touch-sensitive white rectangle is painted around the indication to indicate which modifications are possible. You will see additional icons for other purposes, as well as up/down and left/right triangles for adjusting increments. The existing gestures include:

1. Flick: Slightly move one finger over the screen in a side-to-side motion. Be aware that the monitor may not react if it is touched by another finger or item. A flick to the right or left during playback moves on to the next or previous picture.

2. Slide: You can move a single finger left, right, up, or down on the screen. During playback, you can quickly go between the next or previous picture in full frame view or scroll around a zoomed-in image by using this motion.

3. Stretch/squeeze: while playing back a picture, spread out two fingers to zoom in; while zooming out, pinch them together.

4. Tap: To make a menu alteration, touch the screen with a single finger. For instance, you can adjust a monitor's brightness by tapping the left/right or up/down triangles. When the Touch Shutter feature is turned on, touching the screen marks the focus point and, as soon as your finger leaves the screen, a photo is taken. You

can just move the focus point when you touch the screen to disable Touch Shutter.

- **Setting the Language**

To modify the language of the menus and screens, choose the language of your choice by following these steps:

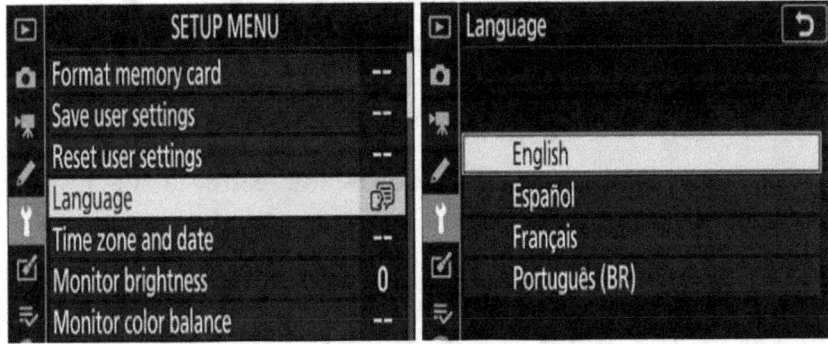

1. To access the Setup Menu, tap the wrench symbol located on the left side of the screen.

2. Select Language by pressing on the language option in the Setup Menu.

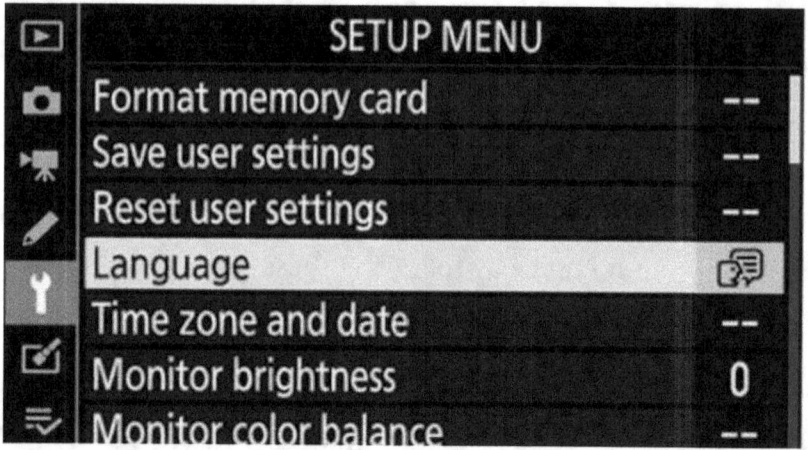

3. Press the preferred language for example the English language)

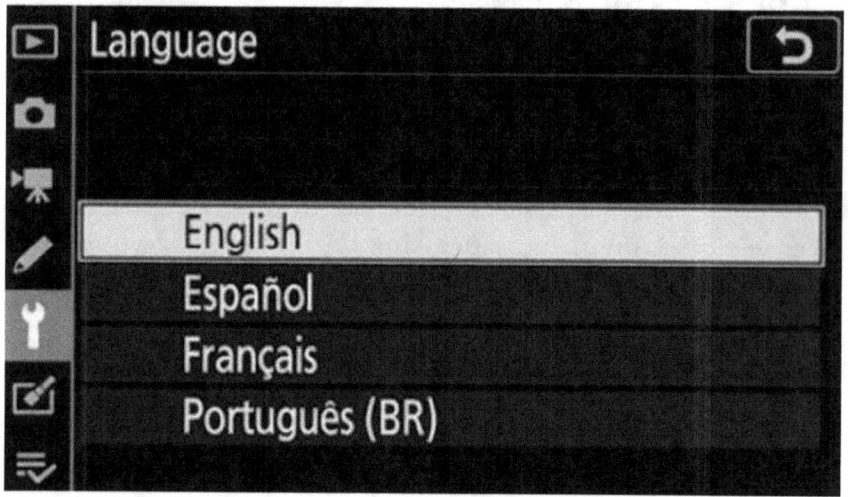

How to Set the Clock

Since the Z7 is often delivered without the main battery attached, the first time you turn it on, you will probably notice an indicator saying Clock Not Set. Furthermore, the "clock" battery on your Z7 may run out of power and "forget" your time, date, and zone, if it is left in storage for an extended amount of time without being charged. Also, when a new EN-EL15b battery is inserted in the camera and charged, you will have to reset the clock. Additionally, it is possible that the camera's internal clock has not been adjusted to your local time when you received it, so you may need to fix that first. The following steps will help you choose the correct time zone for your location:

1. Navigate to the third display in the Setup Menu screen flow

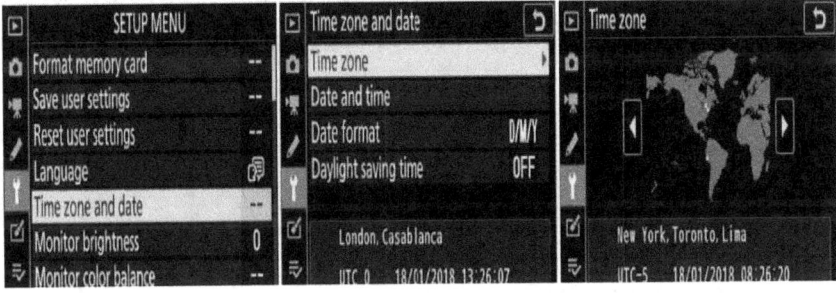

2. To see the yellow highlight of your present location, move the Multi Selector pad left or right. There will then be a vertical yellow strip or a little yellow outline with a red dot. The bottom of the screen will show the current time zone that is chosen. Click the OK button after your time zone has been locked in. After choosing your time zone, proceed with the below steps to adjust the date and time to match your chosen time zone;

3. Navigate to the third display in the Setup Menu screen flow.

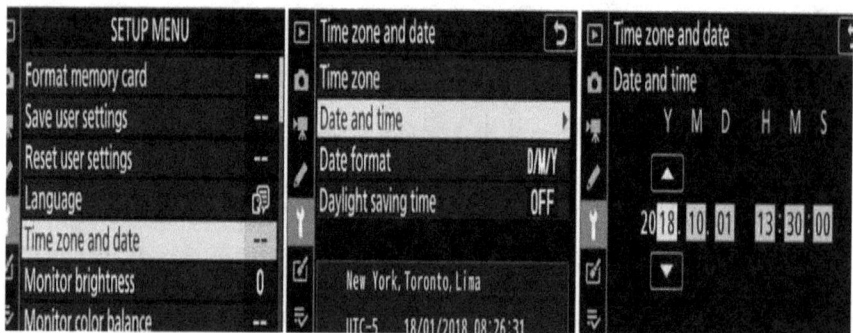

4. Use the Multi selection pad to scroll left or right to move between the various sections for dates and times. To change any of the options, just swipe up or down. The time values are expressed in 24-hour military time. Click the OK button after entering the date and time. The next step is to follow the steps below to choose your chosen format for the date and time;

5. Navigate to the third screen when the Setup Menu prompt appears

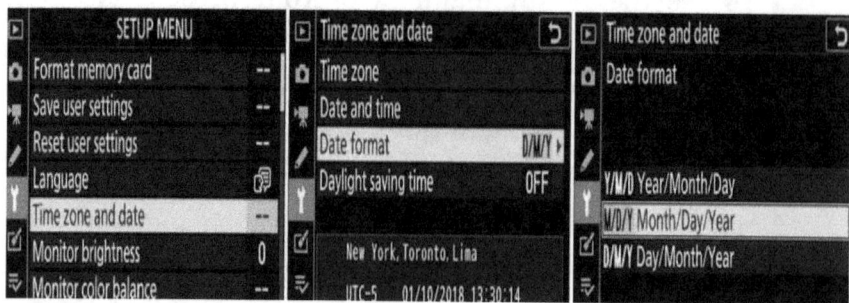

6. Use the Multi selection pad to scroll up or down to choose the date format that you want. Click the OK button to choose the format.

How to Put the Battery in and Charge It

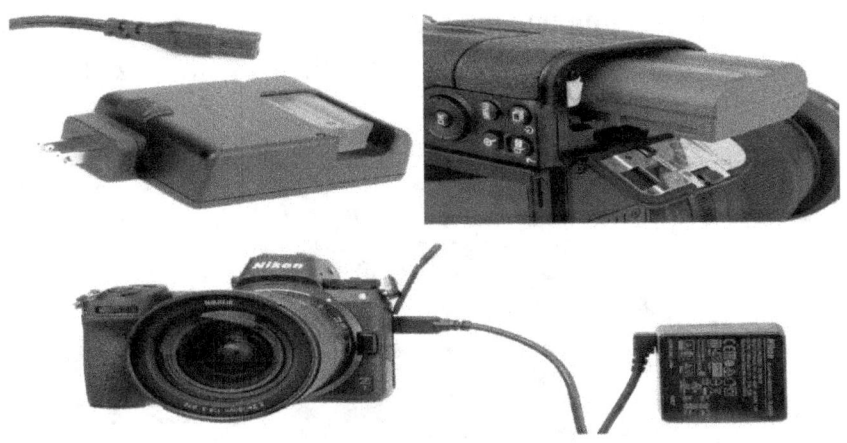

Your Nikon Z7 is an advanced piece of gear and electronics, but it requires a charged battery to work. Therefore, your first step should be to recharge the EN-EL15b lithium-ion battery pack that came with the camera; or any other battery that was shipped with the camera. Note; approximately 400 shots can be taken on the camera, with a completely charged power supply. Also note that whether the batteries are left in the camera or in their original packaging, they all self-discharge to some extent. Even while the camera is off, these lithium-ion battery packs usually lose a few percent of their charge every few days; this is because when the camera is turned off, a chemical process that drains the Li-ion cells' energy continues. It is also quite possible that the battery that came with your camera is at least half depleted, therefore you should recharge it before doing any serious shooting. To charge the battery, follow the instructions below;

1. Note; first a charge light will start to flash immediately you correctly insert the battery into the MH-25a charger. This flashing will continue for about 2.5 hours, or until the status lamp constantly lights to indicate that the charging is complete.

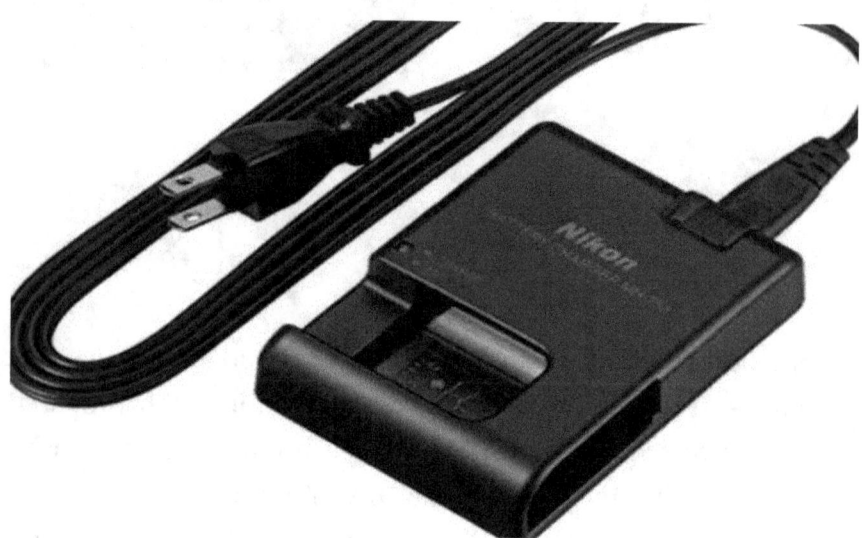

You have the option to utilize the provided connector cable or use the convenient included plug adapter for direct connection of the charger to a wall outlet.

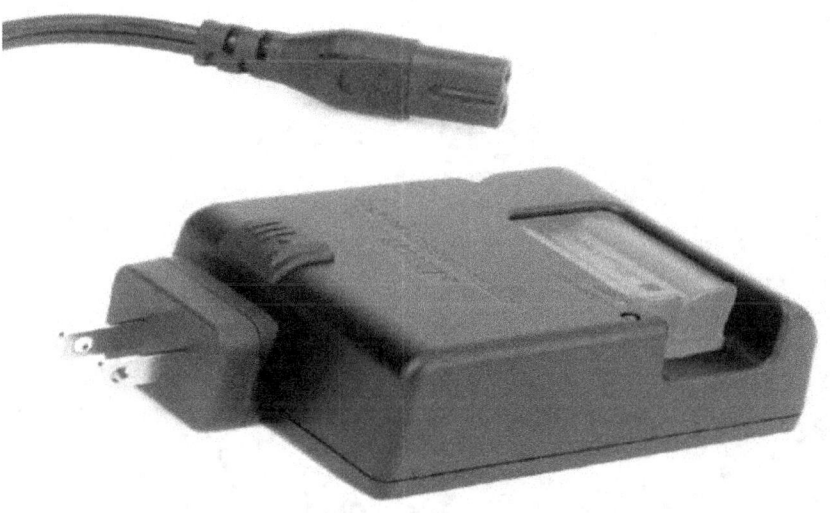

2. Put the battery into the camera by flipping the lever on the bottom of the camera, once the battery has been charged. As previously mentioned, the EH-7P AC adapter can also be used to charge the camera's battery.

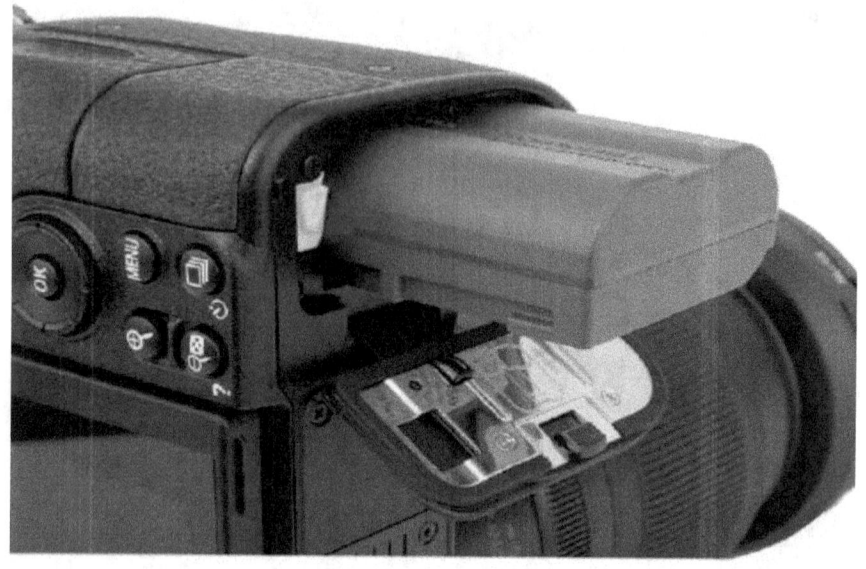

3. One out of these three issues might be preventing your battery from not charging, even after you have plugged it in: a. it may be a new battery that has to be "seasoned" for a few cycles before it would accept a full charge and continue to function; b. It may be a malfunctioning battery. c. The charging cycle for the battery to be fully charged, takes a long time.

Mounting the Lens

If your Z7 is without a lens, choose the lens you want to use and gently loosen the rear lens cap, being careful not to totally take it off. Note: To ensure that your lens is safe from damage, slide it into a space in my camera bag. The rear element of the lens is hidden until you release the rear lens cap, which will allow you to pull it off the back of the lens.

Next, turn the body cap away from the release button to remove it. Note; since it keeps dust out of the camera's inside, you should always attach the body cover while the lens is not on the camera. Additionally, the body cap shields the sensor from harm from things that may trespass.

After removing the body cap, take off the rear lens cap and leave it aside. Next, install the lens on the camera by aligning the lens barrel's alignment indication with the raised white bump on the lens mount. Till the lens is firmly seated, rotate it in the direction of the shutter release.

Turn the lens's focus mode switch to A (autofocus). Twist off the lens hood and remount it with the "petals" pointing outward if it is bayoneted on the lens in the incorrect orientation.

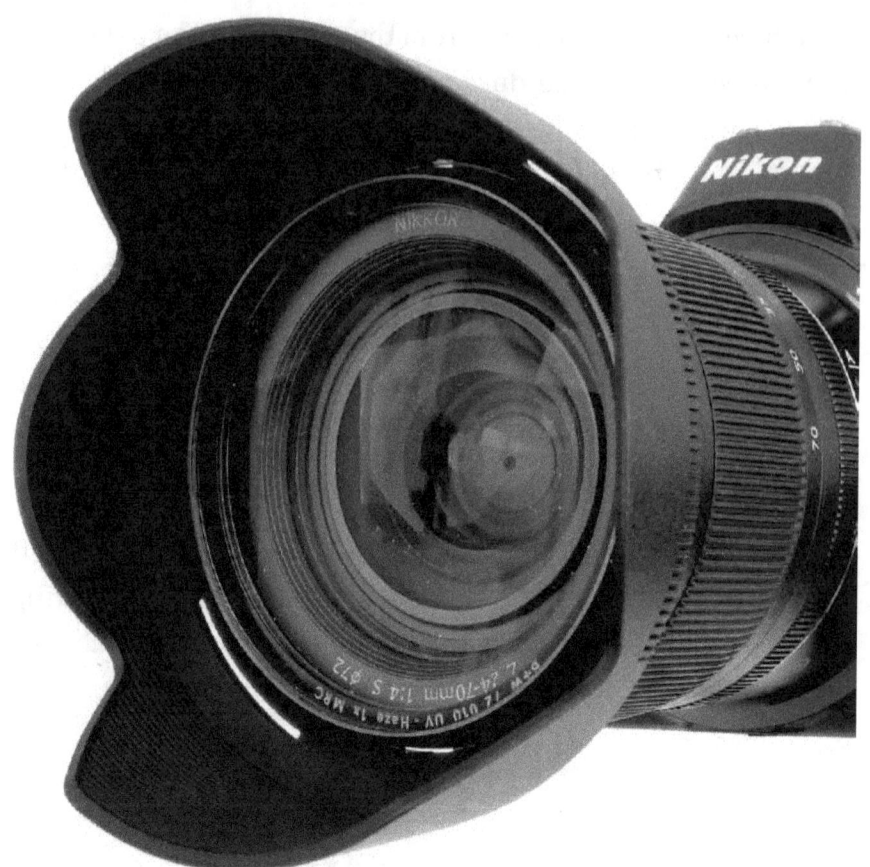

Modifying the Diopter Correction

Individuals with imperfect vision may often get advantages from minor optical adjustments made via the viewfinder. If you use glasses or contact lenses, your correction may be sufficient. However, if you wish to use the Z7 without your glasses, you can benefit from the camera's built-in diopter adjustment, which ranges from −4 to +2 correction.

Diopter
adjustment
control

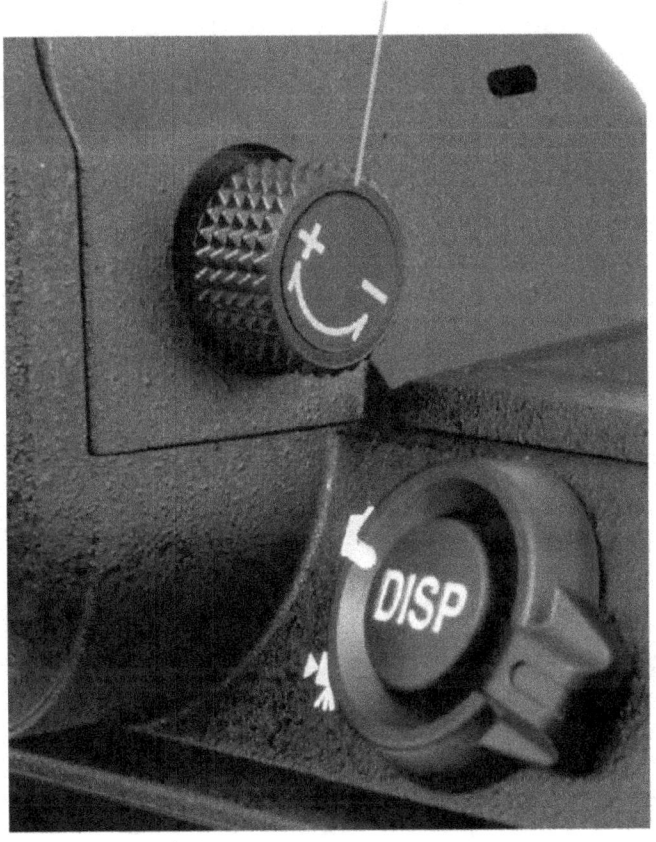

After pulling out, gaze through the viewfinder and turn the diopter adjustment dial next to it until the picture of your topic is crisp. You can save some time if many people use your Z7 and each needs a different diopter setting on the camera itself by keeping track of the number of clicks and direction needed to switch between users.

How to Insert a Memory Card

The memory card cover can be released by sliding the door located on the rear-right edge of the body toward the back of the camera, and then opening it to insert the memory card. Recall that you should only remove a memory card when the camera is turned off or, at the absolute least, when there is no light coming from the yellow-green memory access light, which indicates that the camera is writing to the card.

Place the XQD card into the slot such that the edge with the contacts goes in first, with the label toward the back of the camera. Shut the door and format the card if needed. Note; if you want to remove the memory card, all you have to do is push the card inward; it will pop out far enough for you to retrieve it.

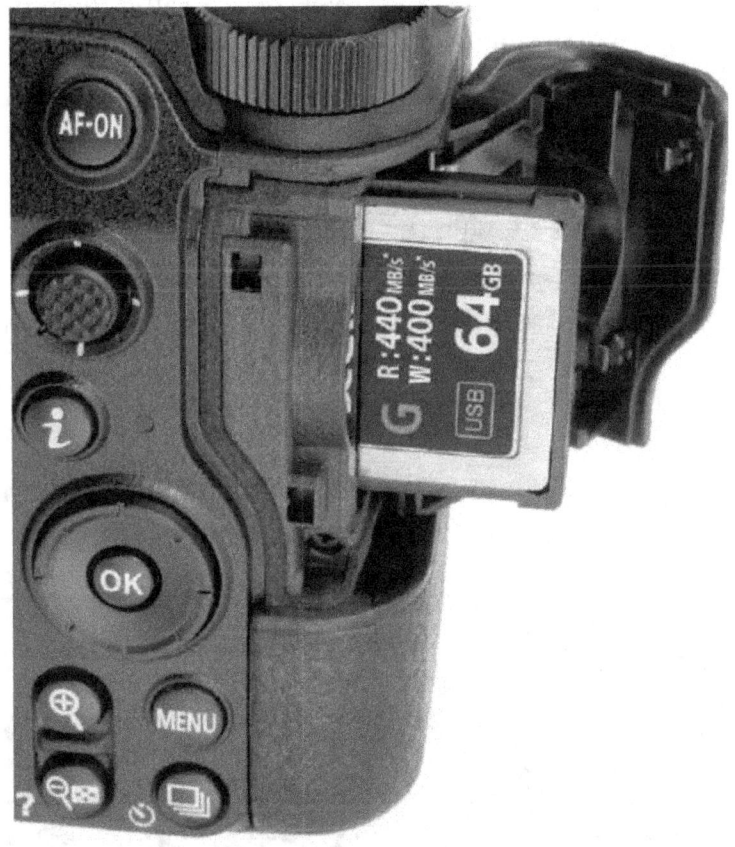

- **How to Format a Memory Card**

Below are the steps to follow if you want to format your memory card;

1. Move or transfer files to your PC: Here, the old picture files will be removed from the memory card, leaving it blank, when you transfer (as opposed to copying) every image file from the card to your computer (either directly over a cable or via a card reader). Nevertheless,

neither the data that you have secured nor the sections of your memory card that have been damaged or useless since the previous format will be removed by this approach. Consequently, it is advised that each time you want to create a blank card, you format the card instead of just copying the picture files. The only time this does not apply is if you choose to share the protected or unerased photos on the card with friends, family for a longer period of time.

2. Using the camera Setup Menu to format: Click the MENU button, then use the multi-selector's right-click menu to get to the Format Memory Card item.

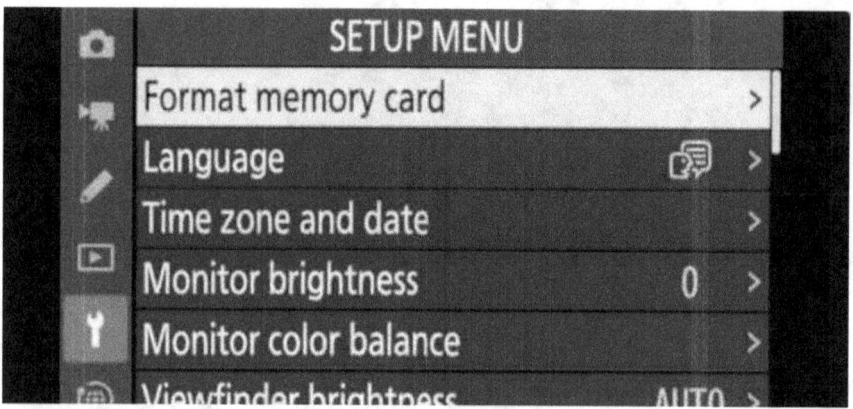

Choose the SD or XQD memory card to format, then click Yes on the resulting screen. You may also reach the Setup menu (designated by a wrench symbol) by using the thumb-pad-sized control to the right of the LCD display. Click OK to begin the formatting process.

CAMERA CONTROLS, BUTTONS, AND FEATURES

Frontside Control, Buttons and Features

The buttons and controls under here are as follows:

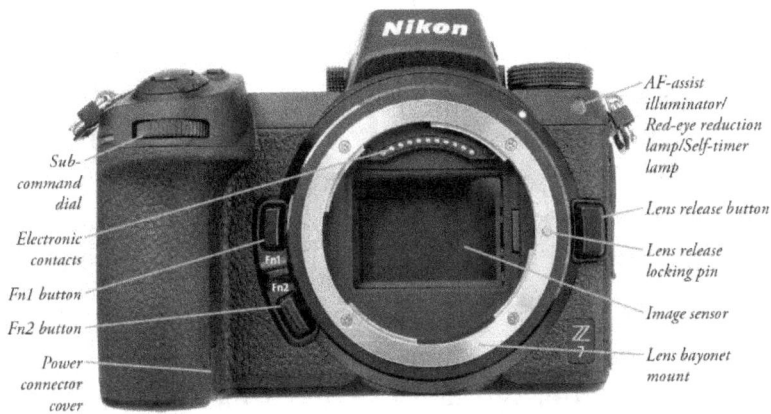

1. Sub Command dial: You can adjust the shooting parameters using this dial. This dial will be used to create one sort of setting, like aperture, and the main command dial (on the rear of the camera) will be used for making the other, like shutter speed, when settings are offered in pairs (like shutter speed/aperture). You can change the default rotational direction, switch between the sub-command and main command dials, adjust the aperture setting on the sub-command dial, and instruct the Z7 to use the main command dial for menu and image scrolling by using the Custom Setting f5 menu adjustments.

2. Electronic contacts: These 11 contact points enable a two-way communication between the camera and lens for features like aperture size and autofocus information. They pair with corresponding points on the lens's bayonet attachment.

3. Image sensor: When the lens is taken off, the Z7's 46 MP sensor is completely exposed. To prevent harming the sensor's protective surface or the in-body image stabilization mechanism, you should always be cautious and never touch or push on it.

4. Function 1 (Fn1) button: The White Balance function is the default setting for the Function 1 (Fn1) button. On the other hand, it can be configured to execute 38 distinct actions using Custom Setting f2, ranging from flash off or bracketing bursts to metering types (Matrix, Center-weighted, Highlight-weighted, or Spot).

5. Function 2 (Fn2) button: Holding this button while rotating the sub-command dial changes the Focus-area mode; holding it while spinning the main command dial changes the Focus mode. The same functionalities that are available for the Fn1 button may also be used to redefine this button.

6. Lens bayonet mount: Each compatible lens has a corresponding mount on the rear that this precise bayonet mount fits with. Four screws hold the brand-new Z-mount firmly to the camera, ensuring a safe but

not too tight fit. In order to prevent even more damage to the camera body itself, their mounting holes are shallow enough for the bayonet mount to snap out if you drop the camera on the lens. Do not be afraid; even with the heaviest lenses, the attachment is more than stable enough for regular usage.

7. Lens release button: To rotate a lens out of the camera, press this button to pull back the locking pin on the lens mount.

8. Lens release locking pin: This pin prevents the lens from spinning until the lens release button is pushed by sliding it within a corresponding hole in the lens.

9. AF-assist illuminator/Red-eye reduction light/Self-timer lamp: This lamp counts down to the photo's capture by flashing while using the self-timer.

10. Power connection cover: This little door flips up to make it possible to insert a cable into the battery compartment in the hand grip from the AC/DC adapter.

Other controls from a side view of the Camera front:

11. Memory card door: To open the memory card door, slide it toward the back of the camera. Insert your memory card here.

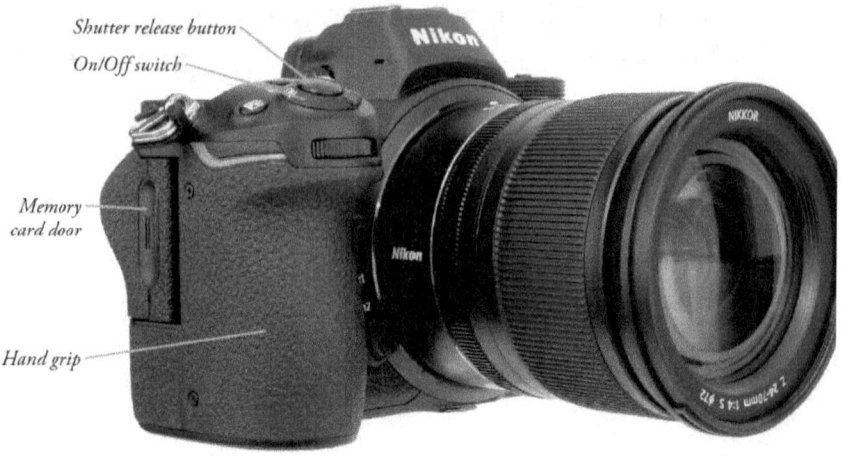

12. Shutter release button: The shutter release button, which has many uses, is angled on top of the hand grip. Half-press this button to lock focus and exposure. If you have configured the self-timer to take one to nine exposures after its delay has elapsed, or if you have set the release mode to any of the continuous shooting modes, press it all the way down to actually take a picture or series of pictures. The Z7's exposure meters may be switched back on by tapping the shutter button, and it also has the ability to be tapped to take a picture or menu off of the back color LCD panel.

13. Turn-on/turn-off switch: Turning on the camera requires moving this switch to the detent.

14. Hand grip: This holds the Z7's battery in place and offers a comfortable grip.

Other controls from another side view of the Camera front:

15. Lens Mounting Index: When attaching your lens, align the dot on the lens with this indication.

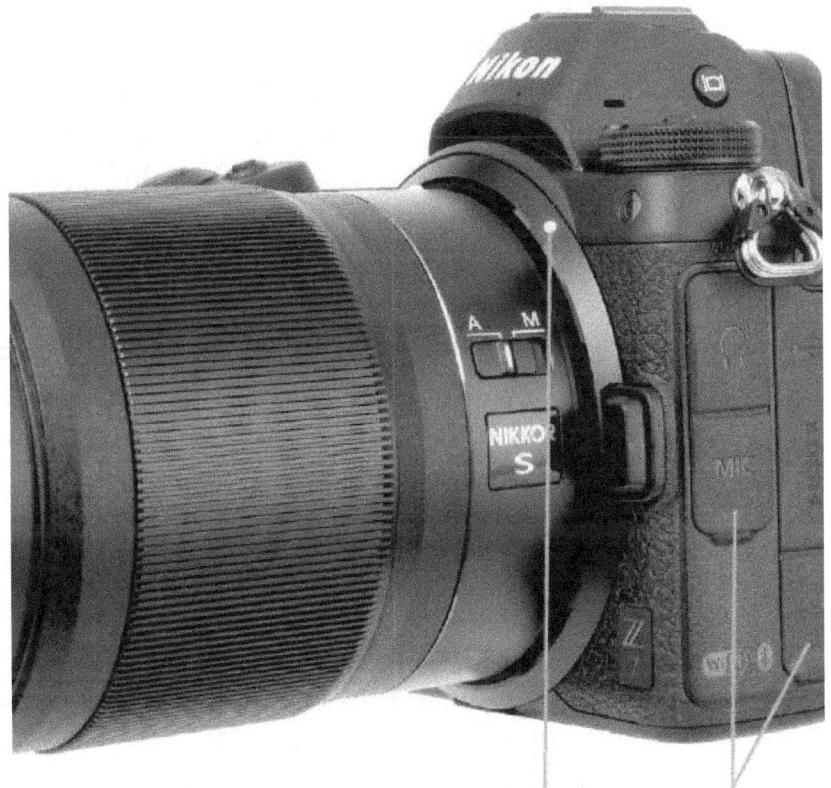

Lens mounting   Port covers
index

16. Port covers: When not in use, these two rubber covers shield the auxiliary terminal, USB, HDMI, microphone, and headphones ports.

17. Headphone connector: To check your sound as you record or to listen to the audio while playing back a video

clip, plug in your headphones or another audio device here using a stereo miniplug.

18. Microphone connector: The Z7 has built-in microphones on top, but you may put in an external microphone, such as the Nikon ME-1, if you want greater quality and to protect the soundtracks of your video clips from sounds coming from the camera and/or your handling of it.

19. USB connector: To transfer images, upload Picture Control settings, or upload/download other settings between your camera and computer, insert the USB cable that comes with your Nikon Z7 and plug the other end into a USB port on your computer. Additionally, battery charging is accomplished via this USB 3 Type-C port.

20. HDMI connector: The Z7 does not come with an HDMI mini-C cable that would fit this connection, therefore you will need to purchase one in order to connect it to an HDTV. The expense is well worth it if you have a high-resolution television so you can see the full magnificence of your camera's output.

Backside Control, Buttons and Features

The Nikon Z7's rear end comprises over a dozen dials, buttons, and other controls. Nonetheless, the following are the important buttons, parts, and their purposes:

1. The Playback Button. To evaluate photos you have taken, press this button. Click the shutter release button or click the Playback button one more to take the picture display off.

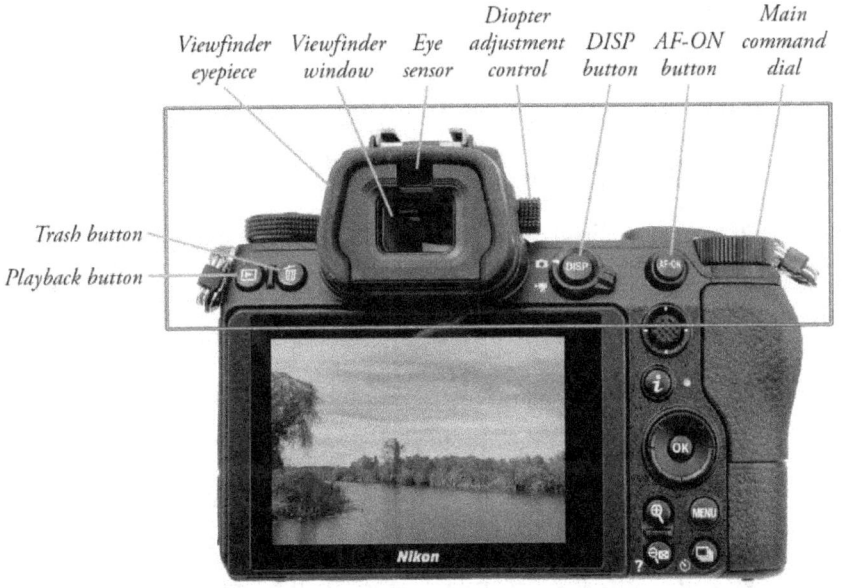

2. Trash Button: To remove the picture shown on the LCD panel, press the trash can button. A screen will appear on the LCD panel requesting that you either hit the Playback button to end the display or press the Trash button again to remove the picture.

3. Viewfinder eyepiece/Viewfinder window: By looking through the 3,690,000-pixel (Quad-VGA) OLED electronic viewfinder, which displays the whole of your picture frame at a hefty 0.8 percent magnification, you can compose your shot. Its flexible rubber frame

prevents scratches to your eyeglass lenses (if you use them) and blocks off distracting light when you push your eye firmly up to the viewfinder. The focus screen region can be seen with your eye up to 21mm distant from the viewfinder glass (the "eyepoint").

4. Eye sensor: This sensor picks up on movements of your eye or anything else that gets near to the viewfinder window—anything closer than around three inches.

5. Diopter Adjustment Control: You can use the diopter to modify your vision by pulling out this knob and rotating it as maybe necessary. You can make modification of −4 and +2 via this control

6. Disp Button: Informational displays on the LCD monitor or viewfinder can be shown or hidden with the DISP button. Use this button to switch between available displays on the picture, video, and playback modes.

7. The Photo/movie Selector: This control allows you to change the camera's shooting mode from still images to movies.

8. AF-ON button: To enable autofocus without having to partially press the shutter release, push the AF-ON button. When used with other buttons, this control lets you lock focus and exposure independently: push the shutter release halfway to lock exposure; push the AF-ON button or the shutter release halfway to autofocus.

9. Main Command Dial: This is the Z7's primary control dial, which can be used alone or in conjunction with another button to set or alter the majority of features, including shutter speed, ISO, white balance, bracketing sequence, and so on. It often works in tandem with the sub-command dial.

10. Tilting LCD monitor: With a 170-degree viewing angle and a 2,100,000-dot XGA TFT touch-sensitive screen, the 3.2-inch LCD monitor lets you see the screen well even from side or slightly above. It offers a complete picture of everything the sensor detects. The camera can be positioned swiveled to provide either low-angle macro images of flowers or high-angle periscope views.

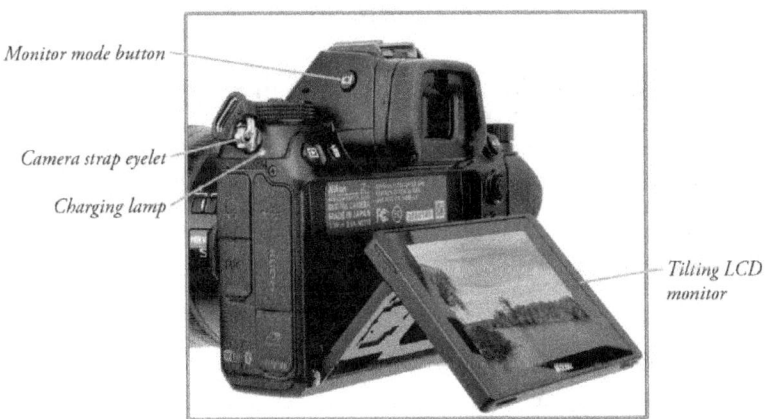

Monitor mode button

Camera strap eyelet

Charging lamp

Tilting LCD monitor

11. Charging lamp: When the EH-7P AC charging adaptor is inserted into the USB port, this LED lights amber to charge the camera's EN-EL15b battery. As soon as the charge is finished, the light goes off. If the camera is

switched on, the charging adapter is deactivated. You can still use the camera even with the AC charging adapter put in, but neither the battery charging nor the camera's powering will come from it. Use the AC adapter EH-5b/EH-5c or EP-5b if you want to run the Z7 on AC electricity. Keep in mind that the camera is not designed to charge EN-EL or EN-Ela batteries.

12. Camera Strap Eyelet: This control has a split ring connected, which you can use to secure a neck strap to the Z7.

13. Monitor Mode Button: To switch between the four LCD display modes, press the monitor mode button. The Limit Monitor Mode Selection feature in the Setup menu allows you to deactivate undesirable modes.

14. Sub-selector: When in shooting mode, you can choose a focus point by pushing this joystick-like control sideways rather than using the multi-selector. When you hold the sub-selector down, it locks focus and exposure while it is kept down. It functions similarly to the multi selector in playback mode to navigate around a zoomed-in picture.

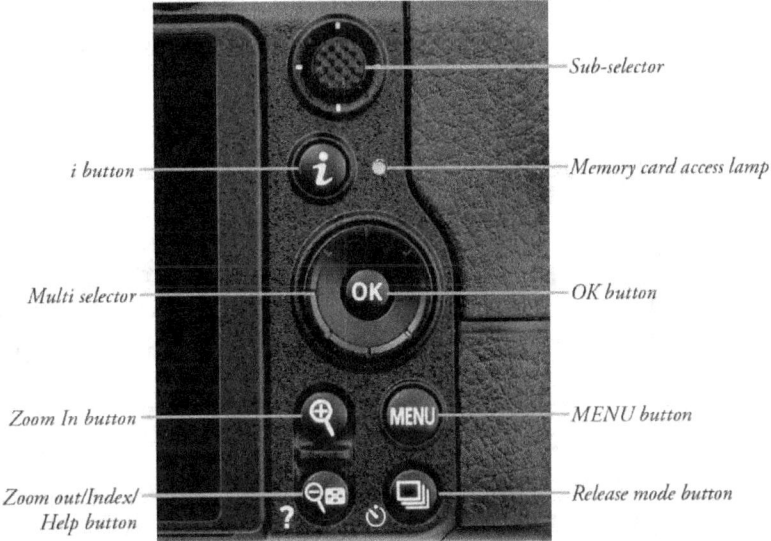

15. I button: This button brings up the i menu whether used in the picture or video shooting modes. The i menu offers 12 modifications in all, but you may utilize Custom Setting f1: Customize i menu to swap out any of the entries you do not use often for another feature of your choosing. The i button has a distinct purpose while in playback mode. Press the i button to pick Rating, Send/Deselect (Smart Device), Retouch, pick Folder, Protect, or Unprotect All while looking at a still picture. You have the option to choose between Rating, Volume Control, Trim Movie, Select Folder, Protect, and Unprotect All when a movie clip is shown in Playback mode.

16. Memory Card Access Lamp This bulb shows that a memory card is being loaded when it is illuminated or blinks.

17. Multi selector: This disk, which resembles a joypad, has eight directions of movement: up, down, side to side, and diagonally. It can be used to pick the AF point, navigate around an enlarged image, crop a picture, or adjust the bias of the white balance along the green/magenta and blue/yellow axes. Using the up and down arrows in menus moves the on-screen pointer up or down; selecting an item and displaying its choices with the right button is done; canceling and going back to the previous menu is done with the left button.

18. OK button: Depending on the mode you are in, pressing the OK button in the middle of the multi selection will enable one of many default features.

19. The Zoom In button: This button is only used while playing back content. In full-screen mode, press it to enlarge a picture; in index view, press it to reduce the number of thumbnails. Note: Similar to how smartphone gestures are utilized, you can also use the touch screen's "squeeze" and "stretch" motions to zoom in and out when in playback mode.

Topside Control, Buttons and Features

The Nikon Z7 includes a dedicated set of easily accessible controls on its top side;

1. Mode Dial Lock Release: You have to hold down this button in order to spin the mode dial and choose any of the settings.

2. Accessory shoe: When you need a stronger Speedlight, slide an electronic flash into this attachment. The many contact points shown may be used by a specialized flash unit, such as the Nikon SB-5000, to transmit data between the flash and the camera, including exposure, zoom settings, and white balance information.

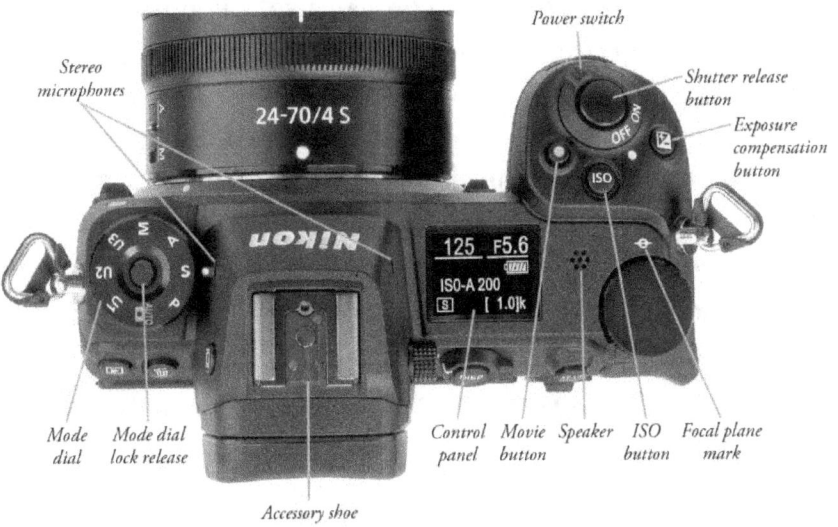

3. Stereo microphones: When filming, this control records audio.

4. Power switch: To turn on the Nikon Z7 (as well as almost all other Nikon digital cameras), flip this switch clockwise.

5. Shutter release button: Unless you have redefined the focus activation button, press this button halfway to activate the exposure meter (as well as the main and sub-command dials that alter metering settings), lock in exposure, and focus. To snap the photo, fully press. When the auto exposure and focusing systems are off on the camera, tapping the shutter release will revive them both. Tapping this button enables the auto exposure and focusing systems to be activated again and removes the displayed review picture from the back-panel color monitor. In addition, you can use this button to leave menus and image review, preparing the camera for a photo.

6. Exposure compensation button: Press and hold the exposure compensation button to adjust the exposure whether in Program, Aperture-priority, or Shutter-priority modes by rotating the main command dial. Additionally, the exposure compensation amount will be shown as plus or minus values on the monochrome status panel.

7. Focal plane mark: Used in situations when an accurate assessment of the distance between the focal plane and the subject is required, this indication displays the plane of the sensor.

8. Movie button: Press the movie button once, to start recording a video, then press it again to end it.

9. Control panel: The status of several camera options and settings is often displayed on this helpful panel.

10. ISO Button: When necessary, press the ISO button whilst turning the main command dial until your desired ISO value appears on the display, in the viewfinder, or on the control panel.

Features underneath the Camera

There is an access door to the battery compartment and a tripod connection socket for attaching the camera to a tripod, under the camera. Other attachments, such as quick-release plates that enable easy attachment and detachment of the Z7 from a corresponding platform attached to your tripod, can be inserted into the socket. The MB-N10 battery grip, which is an optional accessory that gives your camera greater power to shoot longer exposures on a single charge, can also be secured with this socket.

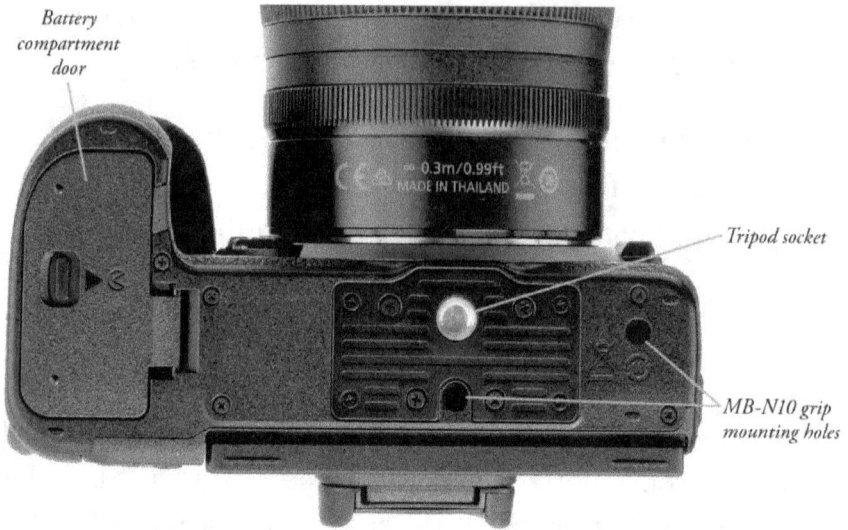

Battery
compartment
door

Tripod socket

MB-N10 grip
mounting holes

The Monitor/Viewfinder Displays

A large portion of the crucial shooting status information is shown on the Nikon Z7's LCD panel and electronic viewfinder. Pressing the DISP button will allow you to switch between the different viewpoints while in shooting mode. When in still picture mode, the shooting information display is limited to the monitor and is available in both light-on-dark and dark-on-light color schemes.

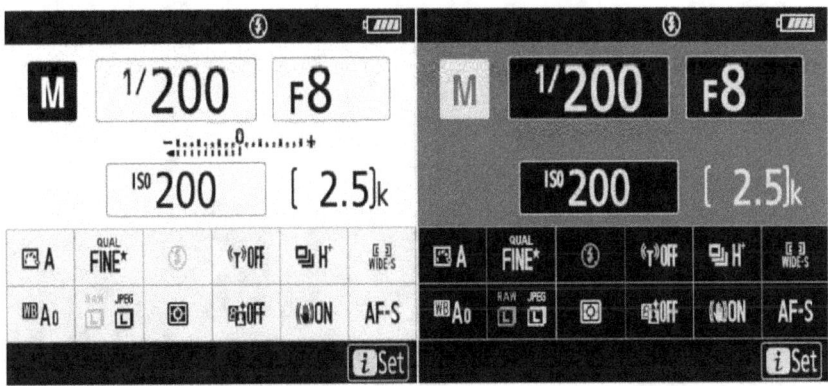

Additionally, when an SB-300, SB-400, SB-500, or SB-5000 flash unit is connected and switched on, or when a flash is being controlled via radio control with a WR-R10 wireless remote controller, an extra Information Display becomes accessible via the viewfinder or monitor display.

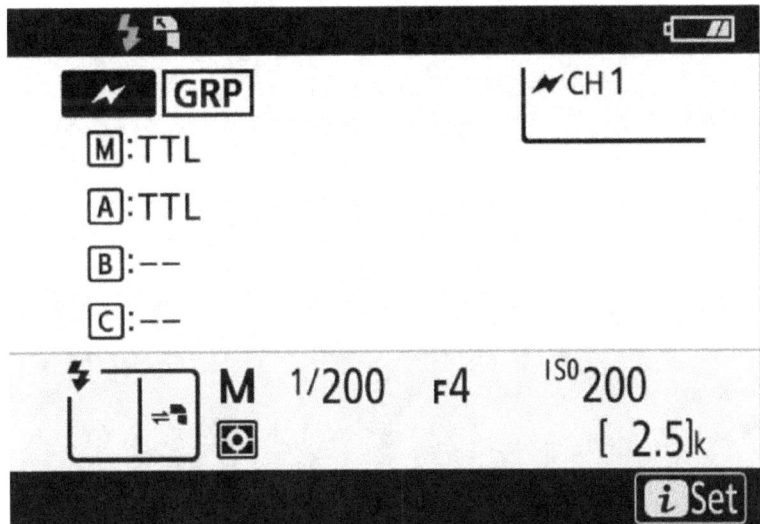

HOW TO USE THE Z7 METERING SETTINGS

The sensor-based Nikon Advanced Scene Recognition System, which measures a large portion of the picture, serves as the foundation for the exposure meter on the Nikon Z7. When using a Nikkor S lens, an FTZ adapter-mounted E, G, P, or D lens with a CPU, or a variety of aftermarket lenses, the camera will adjust the exposure depending on the distribution of brightness, color, distance, and composition.

The color spectrum, brightness levels, and light attributes of every scene are measured by the Advanced Scene Recognition System. For even more precise auto exposure, it then compares your subject to the camera's internal picture database. The Z7's very sensitive metering sensor enables it to do tasks that other cameras find difficult. The procedures to choose a metering mode are listed below;

1. To access the i Menu, press the i button.

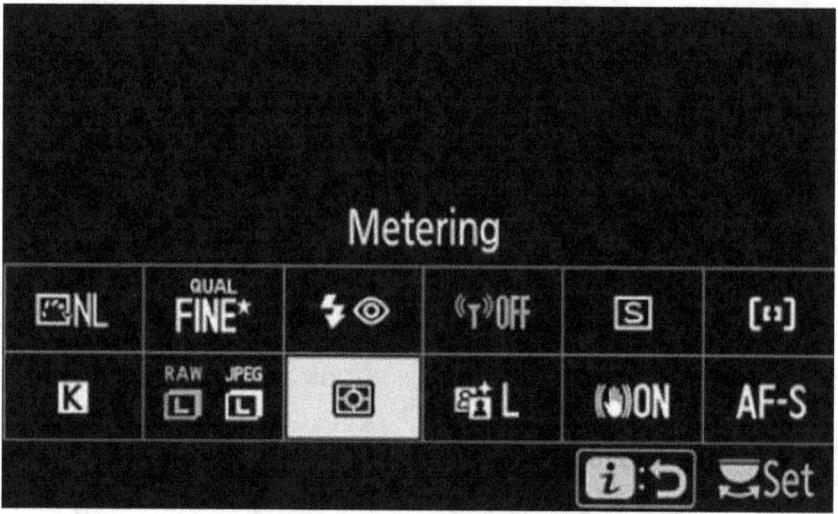

To access the mode selection screen, locate the Metering position on the i Menu (bottom row, third from the left), then push the OK button or touch the Metering option.

2. The i Menu metering mode selection screen shows you a set of four metering icons.

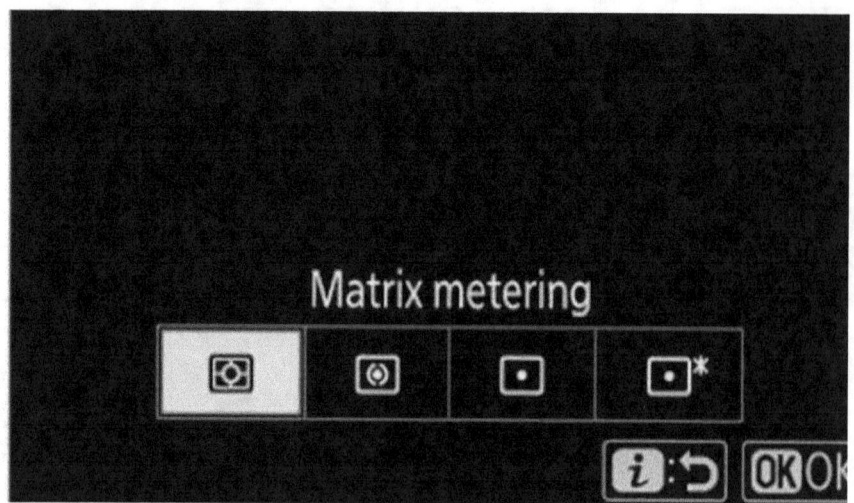

To pick the desired Metering mode (e.g., Matrix Metering), scroll left or right. Matrix metering, center-weighted metering, spot metering, and highlight-weighted metering are your four options. To lock it in, hit the choice on the screen or press the OK button.

3. Once you have chosen a metering mode, you will see a metering sign either in the electronic viewfinder (EVF) or on the camera's back monitor.

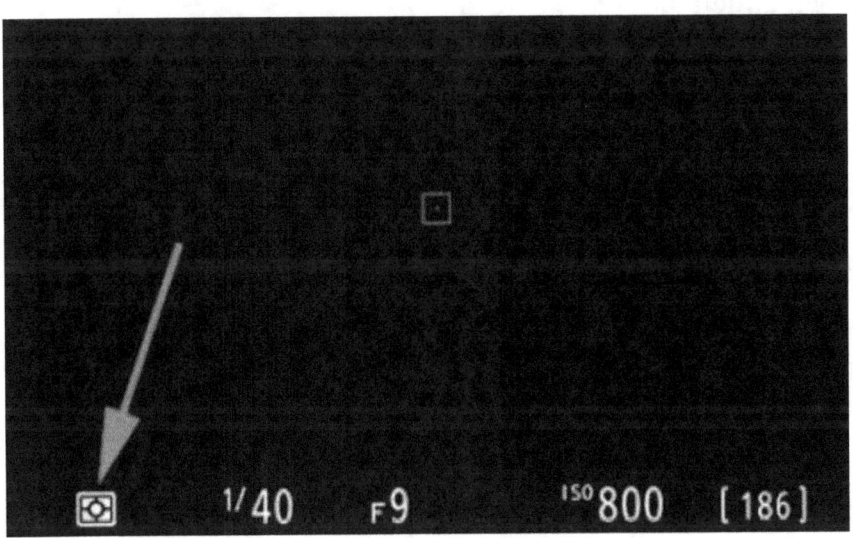

Let us look at each of the four metering kinds now to see one you will utilize most often.

Using Matrix Metering

One of the most potent and precise automated exposure meters available in a camera today is the Matrix metering technology, which is fortunately included in the Nikon Z7.

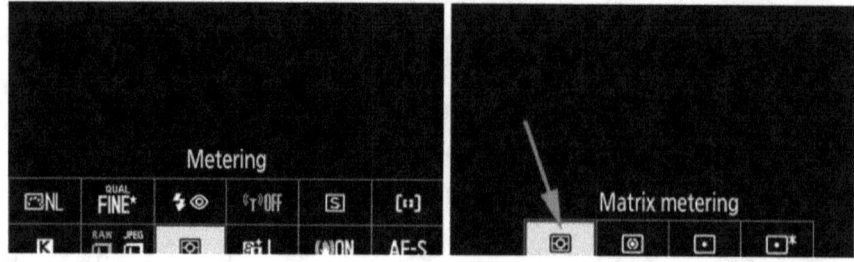

If you observe the image above, you will see a Matrix metering sign (red arrow) in the i Menu. This metering technique is the factory default.

This is how Matrix Metering operates: The Nikon Advanced Scene Recognition System, which is sensor-based, analyzes four important components of every image or video. To find the whole range of EV values, it contrasts the brightness levels in different areas of the picture. It then picks up on the subject's and the environment's hue. It also calculates the focus distance of any S, E, G, P, or D lens that has a CPU installed so that it can calculate the distance to your subject. Lastly, it examines the subject's compositional components.

With all that data at its disposal, it compares your shot to tens of thousands of image attributes stored in its image database, performs intricate evaluative calculations using in-house Nikon software, and determines an exposure value that is typically spot-on, even under challenging lighting conditions.

Center-Weighted Metering

The exposure meter on the Z7 can be changed to become a flexible center-weighted meter with controllable variable-sized weighting.

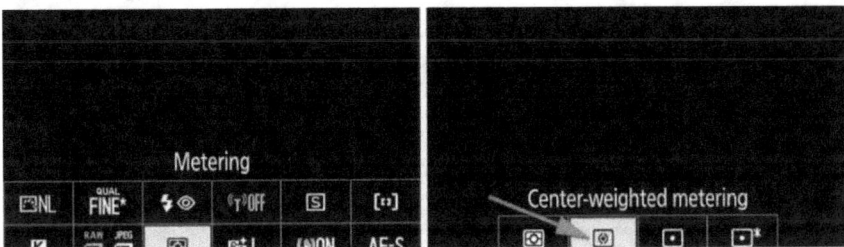

In the above image, the red arrow represents the Center-weighted metering setting. The Z7's center-weighted meter measures the whole frame, but it focuses 75% of the readings into a central 12mm circle.

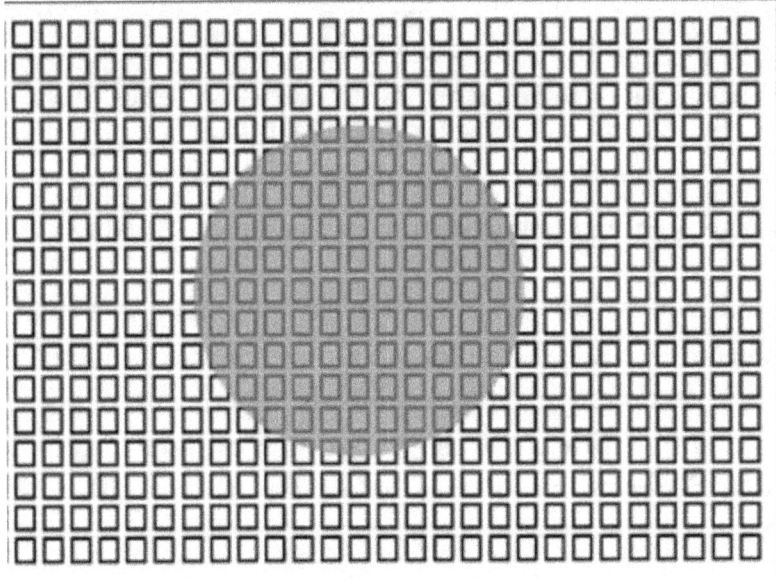

The remaining portion of the frame outside the circle accounts for the remaining 25% of the metering. If you would like, you may utilize the full picture as a simple average meter and exclude the circle.

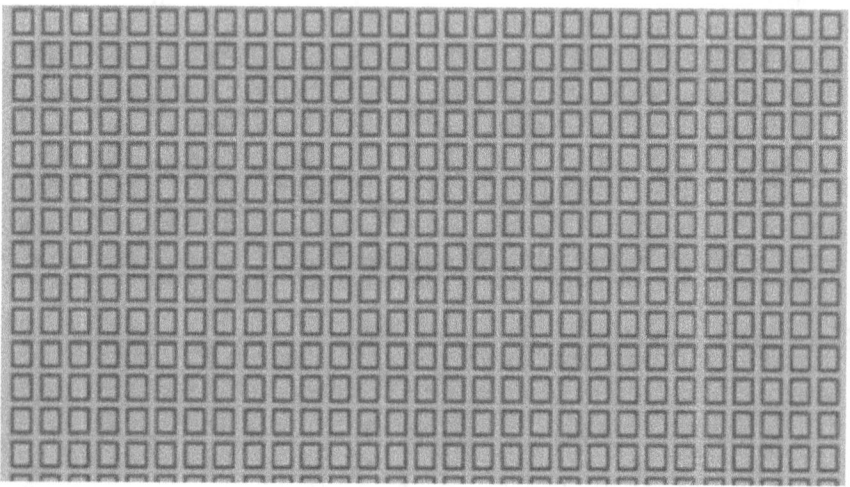

To alternate between using the entire-frame averaging approach and the 12mm metering circle, choose Custom Setting Menu > b Metering/exposure > b3 Center-weighted area. The exposure value is obtained by averaging the light readings over the whole frame when your meter is set to Average (Avg) in Custom setting b3 Center-weighted area.

Note: If you are using a filter with a filter factor more than 1x, Nikon advises utilizing center-weighted metering. Nonetheless, you will get decent results using Matrix metering in conjunction with polarizer filters that have 1.5x and 2x filter factors. Try several filters to see if you notice any issues with Matrix metering exposure while using dark filters; your mileage may vary. In such a case, go to center-weighted metering.

Spot Metering

The Z7 can be customized to suit your demands if you need to get many meter readings from different tiny regions for manual averaging, or if you need to obtain an exact exposure for a very small part of the frame. It is a true spot meter since the camera's spot meter measures just 1.5% (4mm) of the picture.

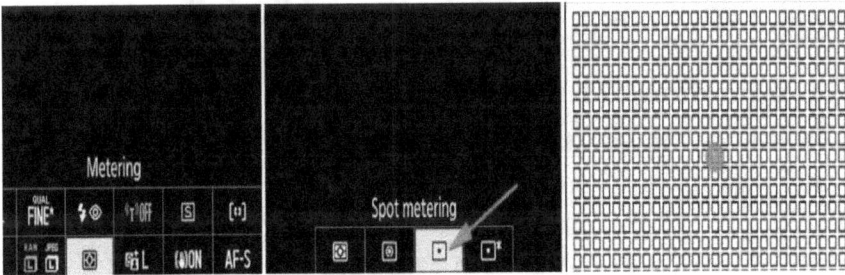

Observe the picture above to see how the Spot metering icon looks like. When using this metering mode, a 4mm (0.16 inch) circle surrounds the single AF point that is presently in use, in both Single and Continuous AF modes (AF-S and AF-C).

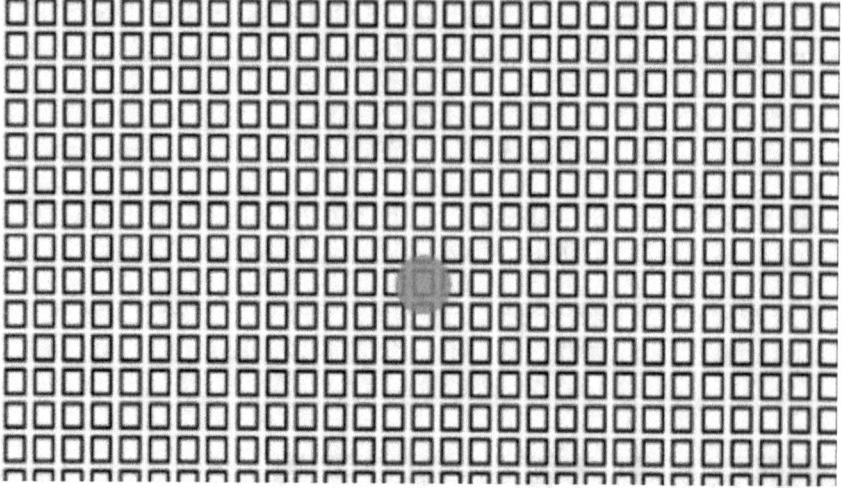

As you move the AF point with the Sub-selector joystick across the frame, the Spot meter really tracks the active AF point within the 493 AF points on the Viewfinder.

Be rest assured that you are receiving a real spot reading when your Z7 is in Spot meter mode and you move the AF point to a tiny area of your subject. In reality, by manually collecting many spot measurements from various regions of the subject and comparing the results, you may use your spot meter to estimate the EV range of light levels in the whole picture. You must choose a meter for the most significant portion of your subject, if the values are more than 10 EV or 12 EV steps.

You can typically get by on a cloudy day since the light's range is usually within the sensor's recording range. A single shot will not be able to capture the whole range of light on a bright, sunny day; to control the excessive light range, you will need to employ HDR imaging or a graded neutral-density filter.

But keep in mind that spot metering often involves trade-offs. You can utilize the camera's multiple averaging capabilities (Matrix meter) to get the right exposure throughout the frame, or you can use a spot meter to verify that a very precise part of a picture is exposed with spot-on precision. You have a decision based on the circumstances surrounding the shooting.

Note; A person standing in the light would often have underexposed shadows with little to no data when spot metering their face. Hence, you risk blowing out and losing information in the subject's face if you spot meter the shadowed parts.

Note: After taking several exposure choices on your own and using your Spot meter to gather precise readings of tiny regions on and around your subject, your subject should be well exposed. Just keep in mind that the Spot meter can only change the camera for the little 4mm region that it sees; it cannot adjust the camera for any other location. Although spot metering is a more exact method of obtaining exposure measurements, it does take some skill to master, so go through this section over and over again.

Highlight-Weighted Metering

Highlight-weighted metering only functions in Photo mode (still photography); it is not accessible for Movie mode (video recording). An example of how this metering mode can be used is; when you have a bright subject on a dark backdrop when shooting in an event, including theater and concert photography. The camera will attempt to compensate for the strong contrast between the foreground and backdrop by burning out or unduly brightening the subject, as most other meter types seek to average the light in the frame. With highlight-weighted metering, you will usually get a significantly better exposure for your subject since the camera will focus more on the subject's highlights than on its darker surrounds.

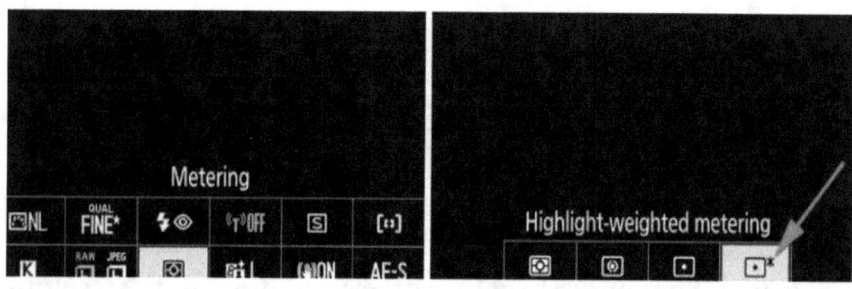

In the image above, the Highlight-weighted metering sign is represented by the little square spot meter symbol with the asterisk in the upper-right corner. To ensure that the highlights of the picture are exposed appropriately, the Highlight-weighted meter has a unique capacity to maintain an appropriate highlight-to-darkness ratio. For example, this kind of metering will offer you a better exposure of the vocalist at the expense of letting the backdrop and surroundings go dark if you are shooting a concert performer in front of a spotlight. Consider all possible scenarios, for instance, in which the subject is bright and the surrounding area is dark. In such situations, the Highlight-weighted meter kind ought to assist you in producing superior shots.

Note: This metering approach can help you maintain the appropriate exposure of the brighter portions when you are taking photographs of subjects that have significant bright areas surrounded by darker sections. The camera will often burn off the highlights in bright regions on dark backgrounds while attempting to preserve some detail in the darker parts. On the other hand, highlight-weighted metering instructs the camera to expose for the highlights while maintaining the darkness in the dark sections. When shooting in this mode, you should also consider utilizing NEF (RAW) mode for the best results. In the dark portions of the RAW picture, there is a lot of buried information that may be exposed using image processing software (like Lightroom). You can manually bring out dark picture detail afterward by shooting in RAW format, which preserves such detail. You can adjust the picture to more nearly resemble what your eyes could perceive during the event you were shooting in RAW mode. After allowing Highlight-weighted metering to preserve the key highlights, adjust the image's balance on your computer.

HOW TO ADJUST THE Z7'S EXPOSURE

The Z7 is a P, S, A, and M camera as well. Furthermore, the Z7 has a completely AUTO mode for those moments when all you want to do is snap quality photos without worrying about exposure. You can adjust the exposure modes by using the Mode dial. Each exposure mode has been discussed in detail;

Programmed Auto (P) Mode

The purpose of the programmed auto (P) mode is to provide emergency control when necessary, but to let you to focus on taking images without worrying too much about the camera's settings. The camera utilizes your chosen exposure meter and handles the shutter speed and aperture for you to shoot the finest possible photos without your help. You can use the rear Main command dial to override the aperture when using this mode.

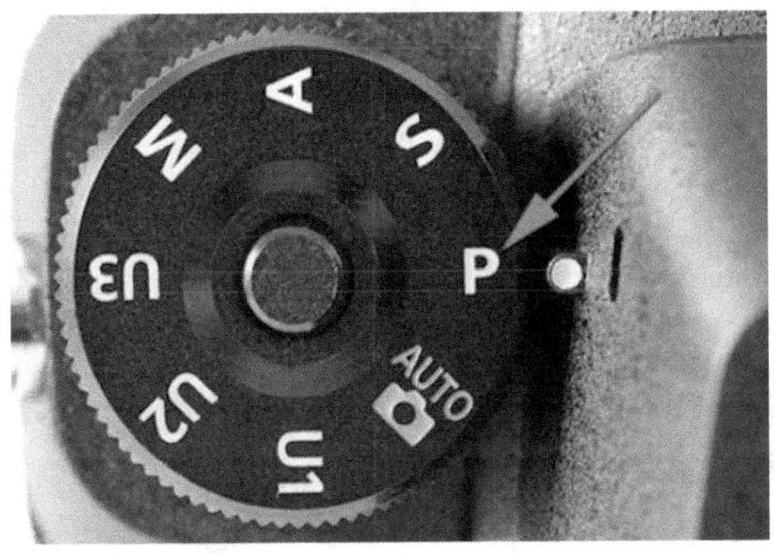

The picture above shows the Mode dial set to Programmed auto (P) mode. Given that it makes use of an internal software program, this mode is known as programmed auto. In most cases, it makes an effort to provide the finest possible photos. The User's Manual refers to this mode as a "snapshot" mode, nevertheless. P mode works great in many different scenarios, such as when you want to take some beautiful pictures, for example, you can focus on having fun at the party instead of worrying about camera settings. P mode is often associated with parties.

Furthermore, if you want to maintain control over the other camera settings while allowing the camera to manage the shutter and aperture, this is a fantastic option to utilize. It functions somewhat similarly to AUTO mode, with the exception that you will override the aperture in an emergency and the ISO sensitivity is not controlled. You can utilize the Main command dial to override camera control in case you require additional depth of focus and want to use a lower aperture. When you do, you can adjust the aperture right away, and the camera will regulate the shutter. Furthermore, there are two components to the P mode: Flexible program and Programmed auto. Aperture-priority auto (A) mode and flexible program operate in a comparable manner.

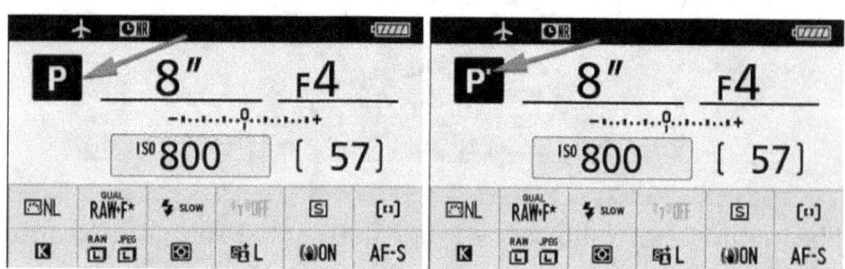

With the Flexible program, the camera recognizes that it is being asked to exit snapshot (normal P) mode and provide aperture control when it detects that the Main command dial is being turned. The Information display panel shows a little P* to indicate that it has detected your takeover of the aperture. It naturally begins to close the aperture as you move the dial clockwise. A couple clicks of rotation to the left, and your aperture is now set at f/8.

The instructions listed above are how to get your Z7 to enter the Flexible program (P*) mode. This is because the Z7 immediately converted from standard P mode to P* (Flexible program) when you cranked the Main command dial; the Z7 was taking care of the aperture and shutter speed before you turned the Main command dial. The Z7 instantly went into Flexible program mode and gave you control over the aperture when you turned the dial. At that point, it alone controlled the shutter speed. Essentially, the Z7 helped you only when you reached a certain level of proficiency in photography, allowing you to practice your skills even faster.

Rotating the Main command dial in a clockwise direction reduces the aperture opening (f/11, for example). Rotating it in a counterclockwise direction enlarges the aperture opening (f/2.8, for example). But if you crank the front Subcommand dial, nothing occurs. It should be noted that in P* mode, the camera will begin to count clicks but will not perform anything else if you spin the Main command dial counterclockwise until the aperture reaches its maximum size. You must make the same number of clicks—up to 15—in order to begin moving the aperture once again.

Shutter-Priority Auto (S) Mode

For individuals who need to manage the shutter speed while letting the camera keep the right aperture for the light at hand, there is shutter-priority auto (S). The shutter speed is controlled by turning the Main command dial, while the aperture is controlled by the camera.

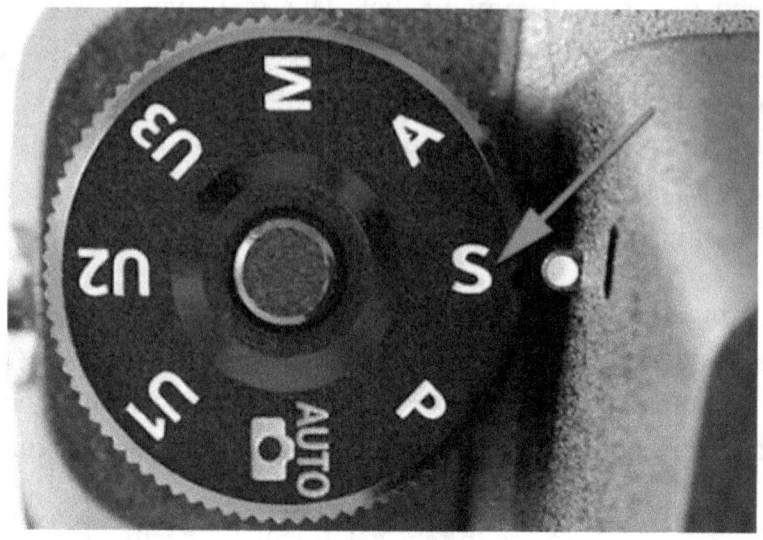

The image above shows the mode dial set to S, which indicates that shutter-priority auto mode has been selected. Keep your shutter speed high enough to take pictures without too much blur if you find yourself photographing activity. The shutter must be carefully controlled while shooting fast-moving subjects, such as sports, air displays, motor racing, etc. If you take a picture of a bird in flight, you should choose a fast shutter speed that stops the bird's body but lets the wings have a very little amount of motion blur.

Sometimes, for time exposures or unusual effects like a little waterfall in a gorgeous autumn stream, you will want to adjust your shutter speed to a slower setting. The camera will blink the aperture setting and display an exposure indicator which shows the amount of under- or overexposure (−/+) in the EVF or on the monitor if the light changes significantly and it becomes impossible for the camera to retain a proper exposure with your current shutter speed setting.

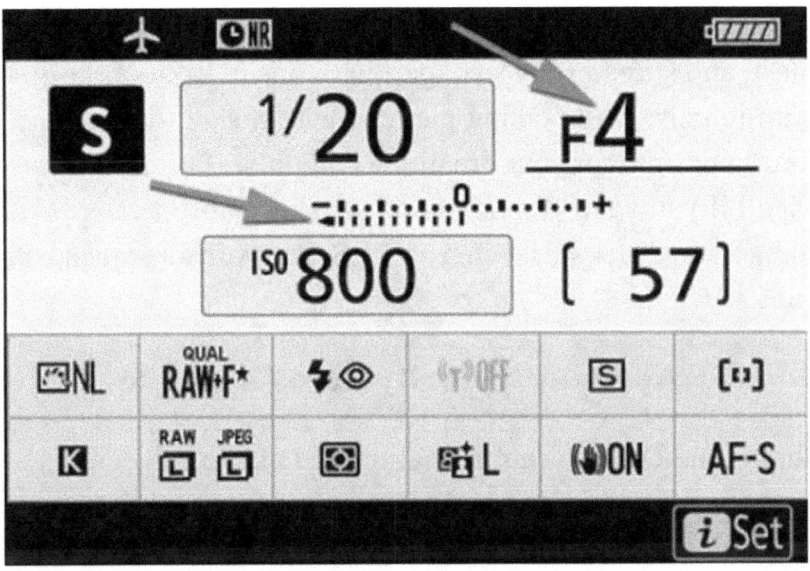

When the camera is in shutter priority mode, the information display will look like what is shown in the picture above. When the exposure is off, the aperture indication (upper red arrow) blinks and the exposure indicator (lower red arrow) appears. Rotate the rear Main command dial to any number between 30 and 1/8000 seconds to adjust the shutter speed. To get quicker shutter speeds, turn the wheel counterclockwise; to get slower speeds, turn the wheel clockwise. If the aperture cannot be adjusted to retain the proper exposure, the camera will blink to alert you.

Note; when the shutter speed is less than 1/60 second, shoot with caution. For many photographers, camera wobble becomes an issue at shutter speeds of 1/30 second and below. You should be able to capture clear shots at 1/6 to 1/30 second if you are utilizing the camera's in-body image stabilization (IBIS), carefully remain still, brace your arms against your chest, and spread your feet apart with one in front of the other. Additionally, while taking pictures with a slow shutter speed, your hands mirror your breathing and pulse. Purchase a sturdy tripod if you want to photograph at slow shutter rates. When using a sturdy tripod, switch off IBIS. You will take much better photos.

Aperture-Priority Auto (A) Mode

Photographers who capture nature and macro subjects, as well as those who want to precisely manage depth of focus, often keep their cameras on Aperture-priority auto (A) mode. The camera is set to Aperture Priority Mode in the picture below.

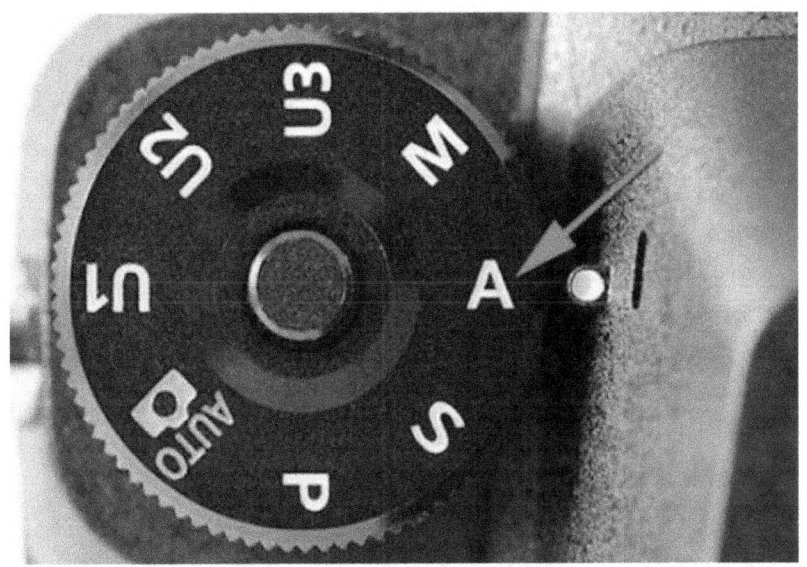

For the best exposures, you can adjust the aperture while the camera manages the shutter speed while in aperture-priority auto mode, or A mode. You can utilize the Sub-command dial on the front to pick an aperture. For smaller apertures (stopping down), turn the wheel clockwise; for bigger apertures (opening up), turn the wheel counterclockwise.

The minimum and maximum aperture apertures on the lens you are using determine the minimum and maximum aperture settings. The range of most consumer lenses is f/3.5 to f/22. Pro zoom lenses typically start at f/2.8 and terminate at f/22–f/32 (e.g., Nikkor Z 24–70mm f/2.8 S lens), although more costly pro-style prime lenses may have apertures as big as f/0.95 (e.g., Nikkor 58mm f/0.95 S lens). The Nikkor Z 24–70mm f/4 S and Nikkor Z 14–30mm f/4 S are two examples of Nikkor S lenses with a maximum aperture of f/4 to reduce size and weight while producing very crisp, low-distortion, and almost aberration-free photos and video. The lightweight and small Z-camera bodies are a good fit for these tiny S lenses.

The zone of sharpness, often known as depth of focus, in a picture is directly controlled by the aperture. Understanding depth of field is a crucial subject for photographers. As a result, it gives you control over the depth or range of brilliant focus in your photos.

Manual Mode (M)

With the help of the suggestions in the light meter, you can adjust your shutter and aperture to your desire when using the manual mode. In the picture below, the Mode dial is in the Manual (M) position.

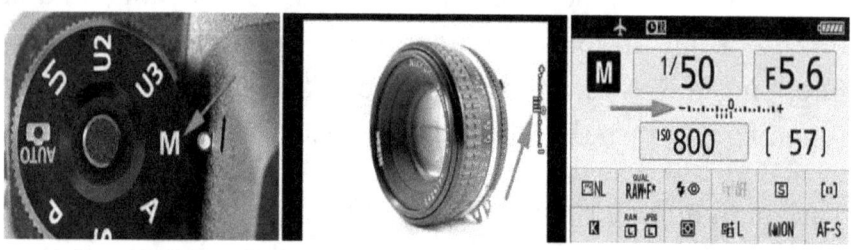

The front Sub-command dial can be used to change the aperture, while the rear Main command dial can be used to change the shutter speed. You can adjust the aperture (for depth of field) and shutter speed (for motion control) in Manual mode. Simply reduce the aperture if your subject requires a bit more depth of focus, but do not forget to slow down the shutter speed as well (otherwise your picture can come out underexposed). In case you want a quicker shutter speed at short notice, adjust the shutter speed accordingly by opening the aperture. You have the last say over how the exposure will seem; the camera will use the meter to propose settings.

Note; you will see the electronic analog exposure indicator which is identified with the red arrow in the image below, on your display.

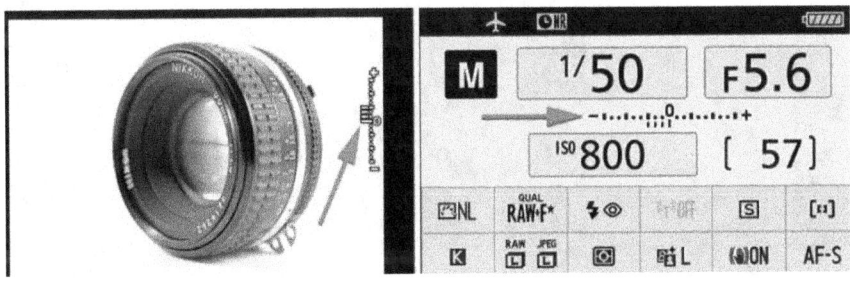

This exposure indication features a plus sign (+) on one end and a negative sign (–) on the other; it can be seen in the EVF, on the Monitor, or on the Information display. On the scale, every dot represents a 1/3 EV step, and every line denotes a single EV step. One stop of overexposure (+1 EV) is shown by the exposure indication, whereas one stop of underexposure (–1 EV) is displayed by the other indicator.

By adjusting Custom Setting Menu > b Metering/exposure > b1 EV steps for exposure control, you can adjust the sensitivity of this scale. Custom setting b1 may be adjusted to either a 1/3 EV or a 1/2 EV step. By default, the camera uses 1/3 step.

On most displays that allow for exposure adjustments, a dashed bar will show up to the left of the horizontal exposure indicator version while you are metering your subject,

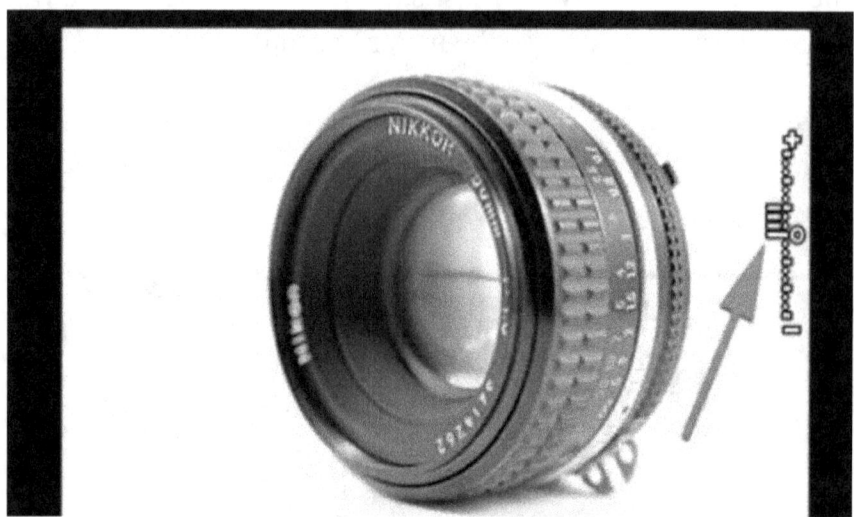

and behind the Information display screen's vertical exposure indication.

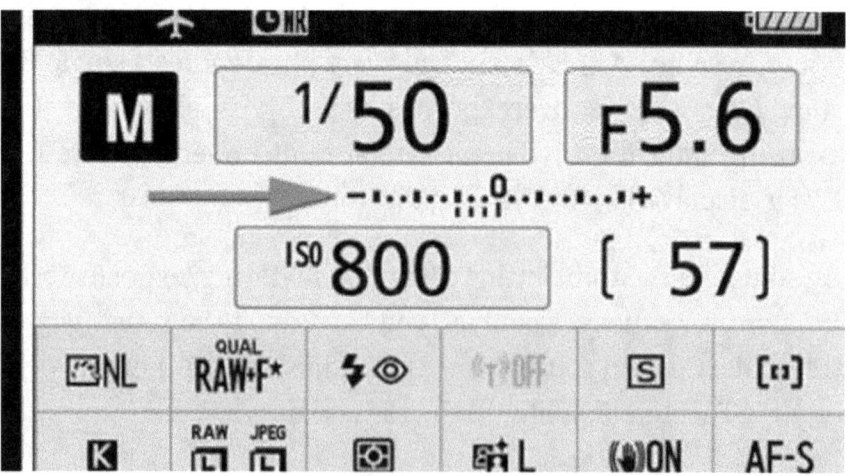

The little dashes on the analog exposure indicator go from the center zero to the plus or minus sides, respectively, to represent overexposure and underexposure. The number of dots and lines the bar crosses as it moves toward either side may be used to determine how much overexposure or underexposure you are experiencing. In manual mode, your goal should be to make the little bars below or to the left of the exposure meter to go away.

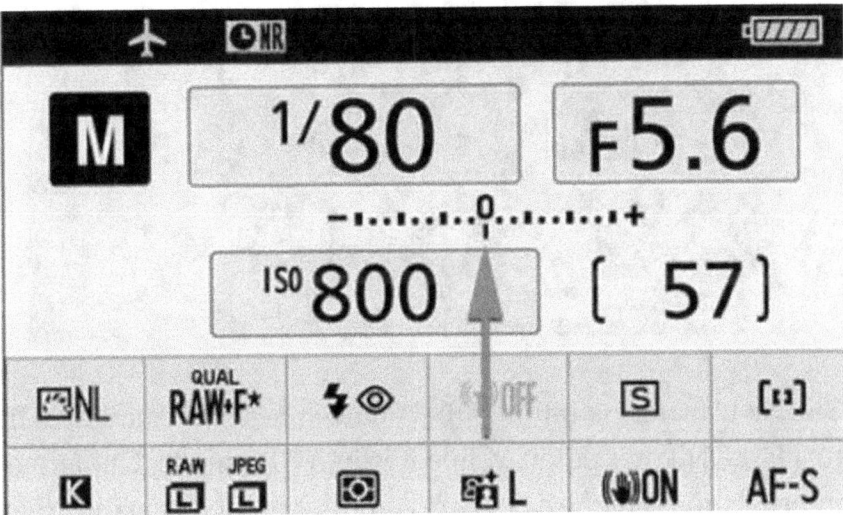

Note: Basically, manual mode is meant to be used slowly and to enjoy shooting pictures. It offers you the most creative control over the image's appearance, but obtaining the right exposures requires more skill.

Auto Exposure (AUTO) Mode

When you want to take a photo without giving the camera any consideration, you utilize the AUTO exposure option. When using AUTO mode, the only things you have to worry about are whether the battery is completely charged and how well the picture is arranged.

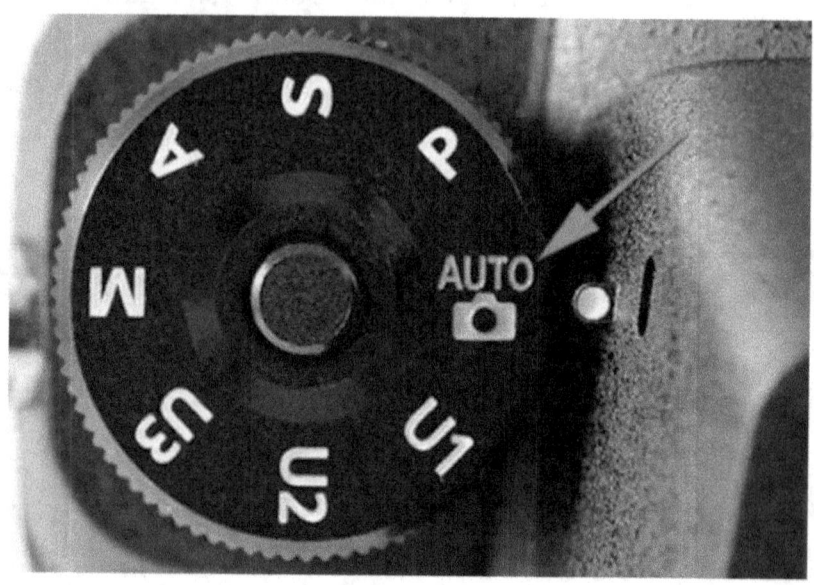

The Z7 transforms into a bulky point-and-shoot camera, akin to a large Nikon Coolpix, while it is in AUTO mode. Numerous internal modes of the camera become automated, meaning that you are unable to modify them as the camera determines what is optimal for each scenario. The following is a summary of several important features that are inaccessible when in AUTO mode:

1. "White balance

2. Picture Control

3. Active D-Lighting

4. Flash control

5. HDR (high dynamic range)

6. Auto bracketing

7. Multiple exposure

8. ISO sensitivity settings

9. Time-lapse photography

10. Exposure compensation

11. Metering mode

12. Electronic front-curtain shutter

13. Focus shift shooting (stacking)

14. Low-light AF"

You essentially give up control over the camera's features in exchange for a "guarantee" that an image of some kind will be captured. When you choose AUTO, the Z7 will often provide its consistently good photos. But in challenging situations, the camera may freely increase the ISO sensitivity and widen the Active D-Lighting range to capture a shot, even if it means sacrificing image quality.

You would also discover that utilizing this mode for a short period helps you become more adept at using the camera's more sophisticated features. Controlling the camera will normally result in better photos, but if you are not ready to give up control, the Z7's extremely effective software will nevertheless assist you.

Note: Without your assistance, the Z7's excellent camera will produce some beautiful shots. For instance, you can switch to AUTO mode merely to enjoy taking images if you have decent light and are not shooting for a business project.

Note; bad exposure warning; the offending setting will blink in the viewfinder and on the monitor if the light changes significantly and the camera cannot maintain a suitable exposure because of your current settings. Also, the camera will show you the estimated amount of EV steps of overexposure or underexposure for the −/+ exposure indication, which you utilize in Manual mode. Please check your exposure before shooting a photo if you observe the aperture or shutter speed setting flashing in any of the displays and the −/+ exposure indicator showing a −/+ EV value.

- U1, U2, and U3 User Settings

You can also change a lot of the camera's settings and store them for later use by using the user modes U1, U2, and U3 on the Mode dial.

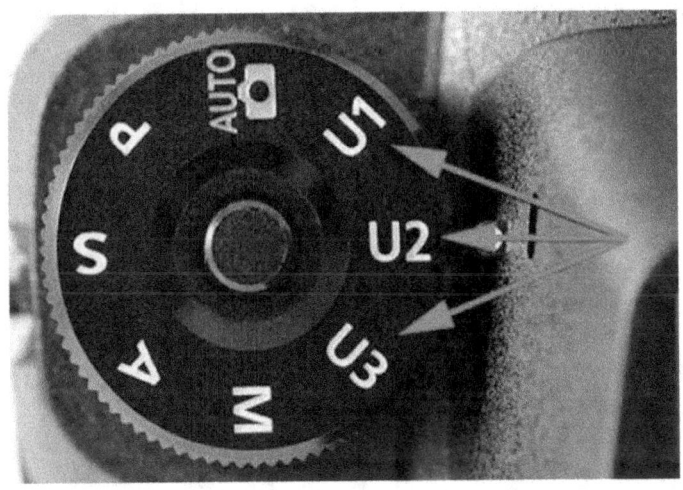

In a manner, you can configure the camera's user settings to perform differently depending on the kind of photography you do. To save the configuration for that particular user setting, first set up your camera's settings and then choose Setup Menu > Save user settings > Save to U1 (or U2, U3). Once your configuration has been stored as a user setting (like U1), all you have to do is choose that user setting from the Mode dial to bring it back into use. This enables you to rapidly move between the three very precise purposes you have set up for your camera.

It should be noted that U1 can be set for the best NEF (RAW) shooting, U2 for the best JPEG shooting, and U3 for party mode.

HOW TO UTILIZE THE Z7'S HISTOGRAM SETTINGS

We can be sure to take high-quality pictures with the Z7's exposure meter/histogram combo and the high-resolution monitor on the rear of the camera, which allows us to zoom in on our subjects. The histogram may have equal or more significance than the exposure meter. The histogram confirms that the exposure is correct, while the meter sets up the camera for the exposure.

Even if the readout on your exposure meter stopped functioning, you could still use the histogram to get precise exposures. Together, the exposure meter and histogram ensure that your photography endeavors provide outstanding outcomes. Here are the several types of histograms:

1. Live Luminance Histogram: When this is in use, a live brightness histogram will be displayed on the monitor and in the EVF of the Z7.

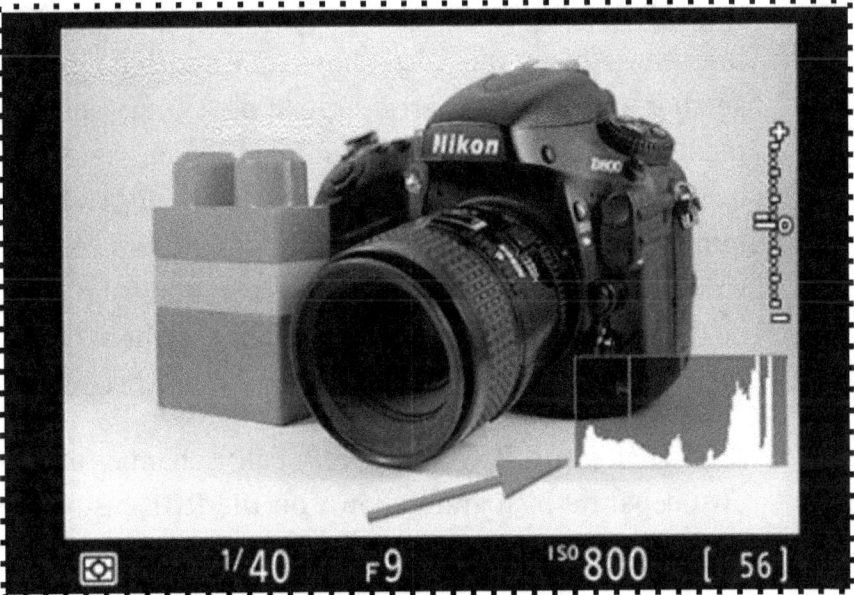

The picture above shows a simple luminance histogram, which is a weighted representation of a scene's brightness and color based on how the human eye interprets light. Here, the exposure of the current image's you are working on, is reflected in the live histogram. You can immediately see how the exposure levels are changing as you adjust them, giving you reassurance when your exposure is appropriate or caution when it is not. The way the luminance histogram works is that it combines the red, green, and blue channels to represent the perceived brightness, or luminosity. But then, the brightness histogram employs a certain color value weighting scheme to approximate the light that is seen by the human eye. The brightness histogram is highly weighted toward green since green is the color that the human eye perceives the best. The brightness histogram also shows red and blue, but in smaller amounts (59 percent green plus 30 percent red plus 11 percent blue equals luminance). The perceived brightness is measured in 256 levels (0–255) via the luminance histogram. This method provides a realistic view of the blended color levels in actual photos. It could be the ideal histogram for you to utilize as it more closely mimics how our eyes truly perceive color and brightness.

2. RGB Histogram Playback: Every color channel has its own separate histogram shown on the RGB histogram screen.

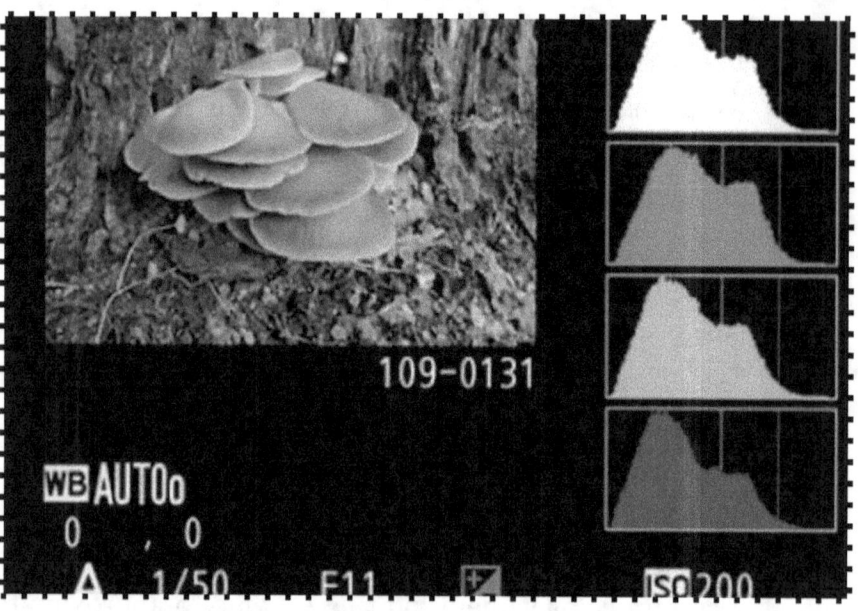

Note; the histograms here are not real-time/live. They appear after you snap the photo so you would be able to check the exposure of the image. In this mode, a luminance histogram is located at the top, which is followed by individual red, green, and blue (RGB) histogram channels. You must tick the item under Playback Menu > Playback display settings > RGB histogram if your camera is not displaying the RGB histogram. The RGB histogram screen can be found by displaying a picture on the monitor and using the Multi selection pad to scroll up or down when this option is enabled or off. Examining the RGB histogram is important, to determine if any particular color channel has completely lost information in the bright or dark regions.

3. The Playback Luminance Histogram: This includes picture data in addition to a significantly wider brightness histogram. This histogram is not real-time. It appears after you snap the photo so you will be able to check the exposure of the image.

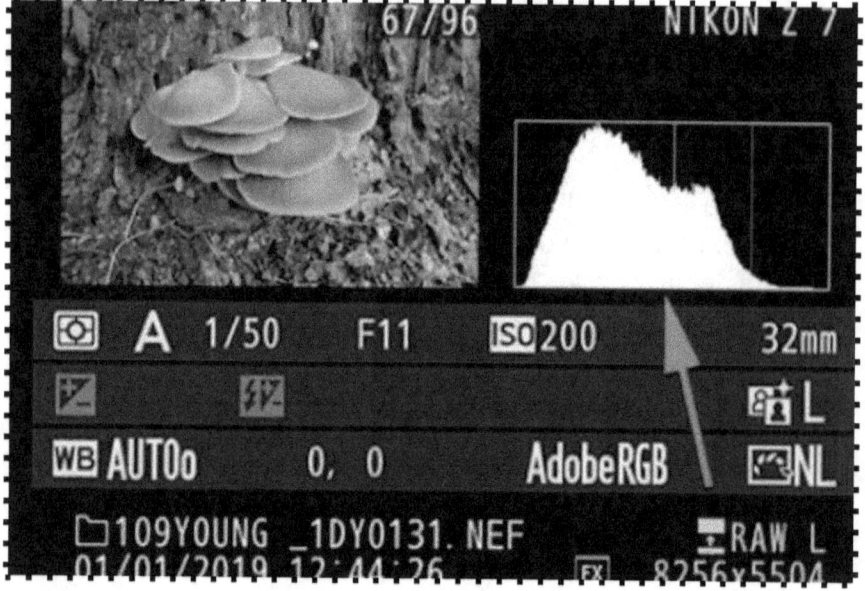

You should select the item under Playback Menu > Playback display settings > Overview if your camera is not displaying the Luminance histogram panel. You can discover the Overview screen by playing an image on the Monitor and using the Multi selection pad to scroll up or down when this option is enabled or off.

Understanding the Histogram

A broad range of light values can be recorded by the Z7's image sensor. Unfortunately, many of the higher contrast things we photograph include more light range than the camera can capture in one exposure, despite the Z7's enormous potential dynamic range.

Making use of the Z7's histogram panels will ensure a much larger proportion of properly exposed photos. It is worthwhile to invest effort in comprehending the histogram. It is not as hard as it seems. To assess how well you have recorded the light in the scene in front of your lens, let us take a closer look at the histogram.

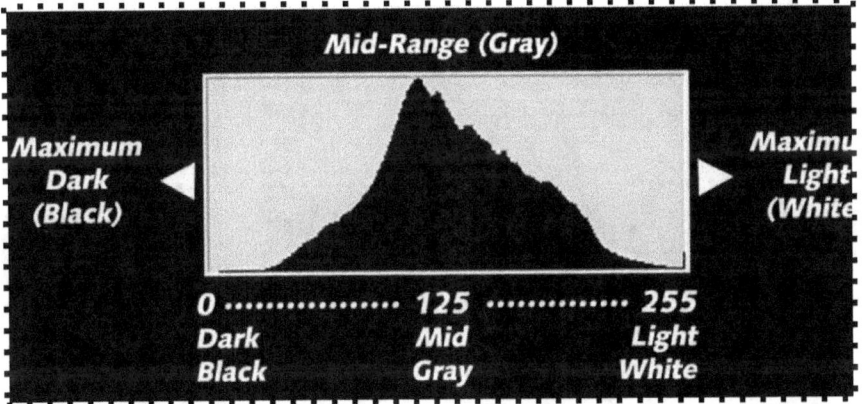

Keep in mind that the image's gray rectangle region depicts an in-camera histogram. The greatest range of light values that your camera is capable of capturing is represented by the histogram, which is essentially a graph with 256 steps (0 being pure black and 255 being pure white). The midrange values, which stand for intermediate hues like grays, light browns, and greens, are located in the center of the histogram. The image histogram detail is contained in values that are slightly above zero to slightly below 255. The real histogram often resembles a mountain peak or a group of peaks, with the peak representing a given hue growing in height as more of that color is present. The graph can sometimes have many peaks or be flattened, with a rounder top. The utmost dark values that your camera is capable of recording will be shown on the left side of the histogram. The highest light value that your camera is capable of capturing will be shown on the right side. The bright values on either end of the histogram (0 or 255) are devoid of information. They might be all white (255) or entirely black (0). The number of distinct colors is represented by the height of the histogram, which resembles the top of a mountain. This number is for your knowledge only since there is no easy way to alter it in-camera other than switching to a Picture alter with a more or less saturated hue.

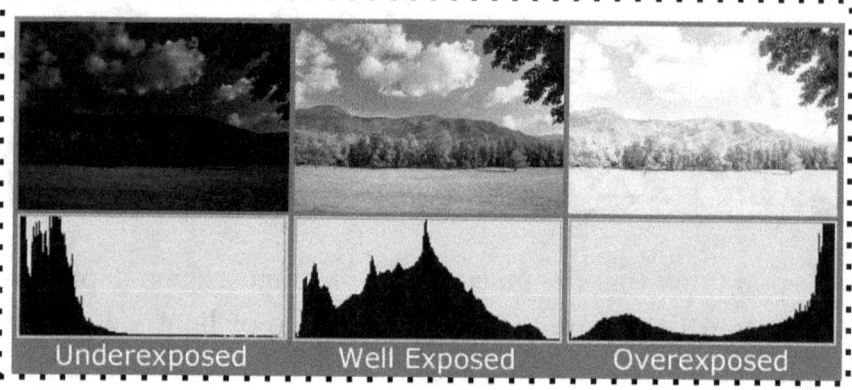

Three histogram scenarios are displayed in the picture above: one is underexposed, one is well exposed, and one is overexposed. Since you do have much more influence on the left and right side values of the histogram (dark vs bright), you could be primarily interested in them. This is easy to understand since the vertical scale of the histogram, which represents the mountain peaks and valleys, corresponds to the quantity of color information, while the horizontal scale represents the image's brightness and darkness. For capturing pictures, the horizontal scale's left (dark) and right (light) orientations are crucial. The light values will be cut off on the left side of the picture if it is too dark, and on the right side if it is too bright.

In the picture above, see how the well-exposed histogram's two edges almost meet the histogram window's horizontal edges. Lastly, take note of the clipped and pushed toward the right overexposed histogram. Note that an accurate exposure can also be achieved with a histogram that does not span the whole window. The histogram may be rather thin when there is a very small light range. The important thing to keep in mind is that a histogram that is clipped and packed all the way to the left indicates that part or all of the picture is noticeably too dark. Some or all of the picture is noticeably too light if the histogram is cropped and pushed all the way to the right. It is crucial that you make an effort to center the histogram without cutting any edges. Because the light range is often too large for the sensor or histogram window to encompass, this is not always practicable. You can change the exposure and take another picture if you take one and the histogram shifts to the left or right. You have to choose whether the area of the picture is more crucial—the bright or dark values—and expose for those values if there is too much light to enable the histogram to be centered.

Note: Only the first exposure should be obtained using the light meter on the camera. Next, you can use the histogram to determine if the image's light range falls within the sensor's restricted range. If you desire, you can use Manual mode or adjust the exposure by using the +/− Exposure compensation button if the histogram seems clipped to the left or right. Once your light meter has brought you near, use the histogram to fine-tune. You can position the light range of your photos with a great deal of control if you become proficient with the histogram.

Highlights (Blink) Mode

In addition to the histogram, you can also utilize various viewing modes for the Monitor, including the Highlights (blink) mode for blown-out highlights (check the box next to Highlights in the Playback Menu > Playback display choices).

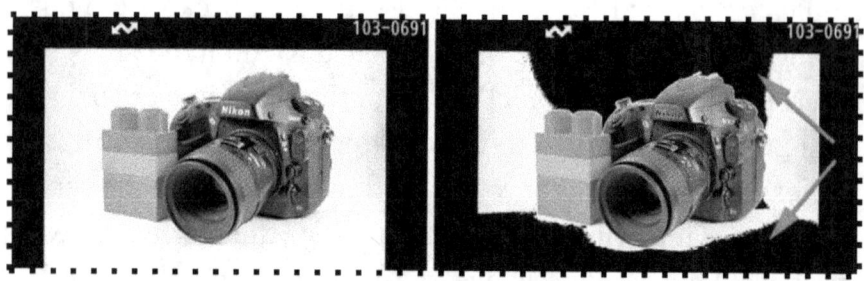

Note; as can be observed by looking at the white backdrop of the first image in the illustration above, the blink mode will cause your image to flash in the blown-out highlight regions from bright to dark in the. For fast photography, this white-to-black flashing is pretty helpful. It is a crude approximation of a histogram with the highlight value cut. Controlling your exposures effectively would be achieved by using the light meter, histogram, and Highlights (blink) setting on your camera.

THE Z7 FOCUS MODES

Every time you use your camera, you will have to deal with the Focus modes. The camera's focus and location are determined by these crucial features. You can utilize the Photo and Movie Shooting Menus, the i Menu, or a designated camera button to access the Focus and AF-area modes. Let us start by examining how to use the i Menu to access the modes.

Accessing the Focus and AF Modes with the i Menu

To get to the Focus and AF-area modes from the i Menu, use these steps:

1. To access the i Menu, press the i button.

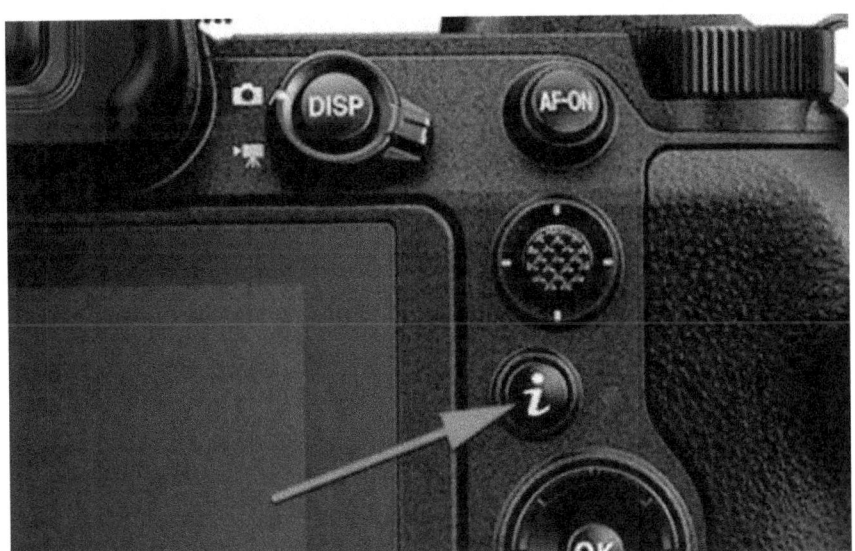

2. Scroll down to the bottom row of the list and navigate ,
   to find the Focus mode

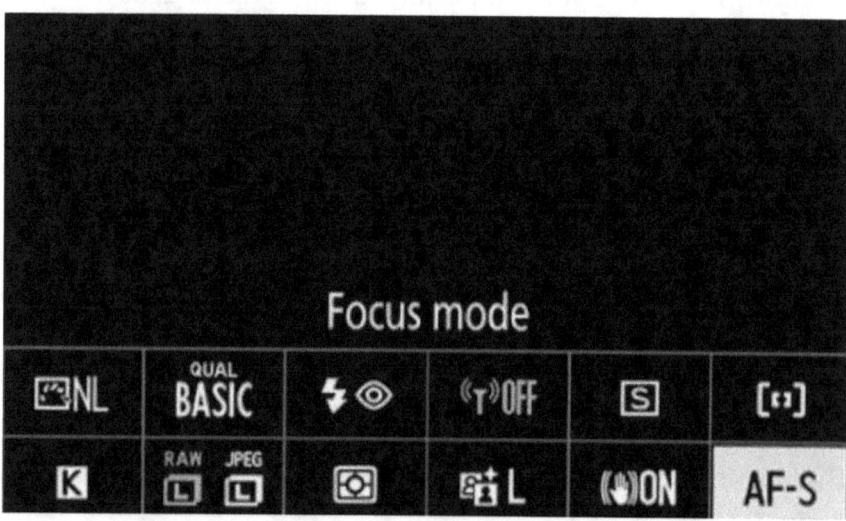

3. Look carefully, you will see the AF-area mode point on
   the extreme right of the top row, on the display.

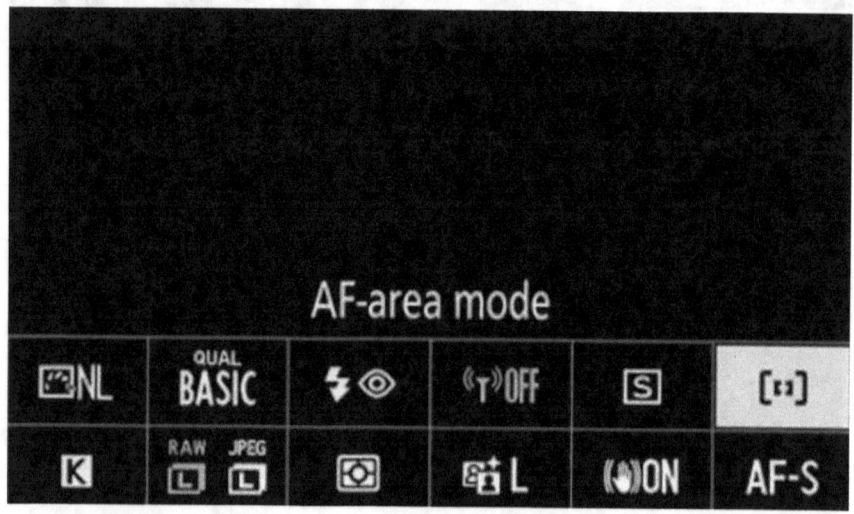

Using the Assigned Button to Access the Focus And AF Mode

To set Focus mode or AF-area mode to one of the camera's buttons, follow these steps:

1. From the Custom Setting Menu, choose f Controls, then scroll to the right.

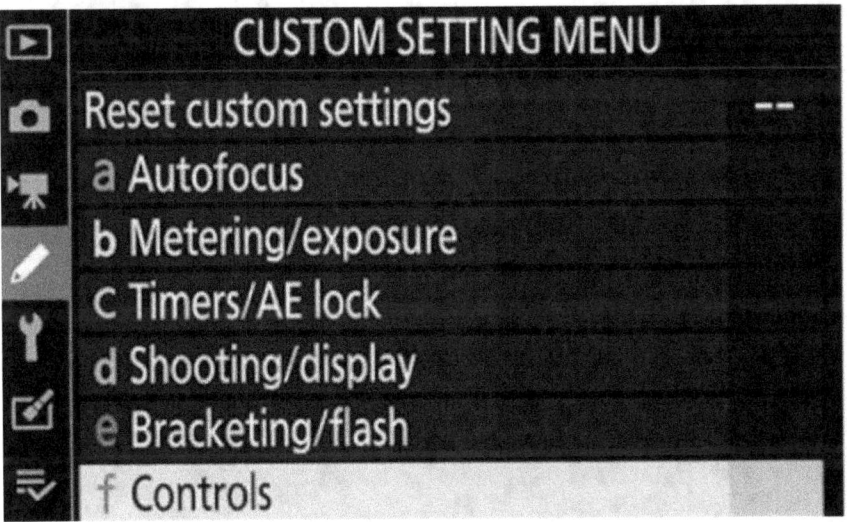

2. From the f Controls menu, choose f2 Custom control assignment, then scroll to the right.

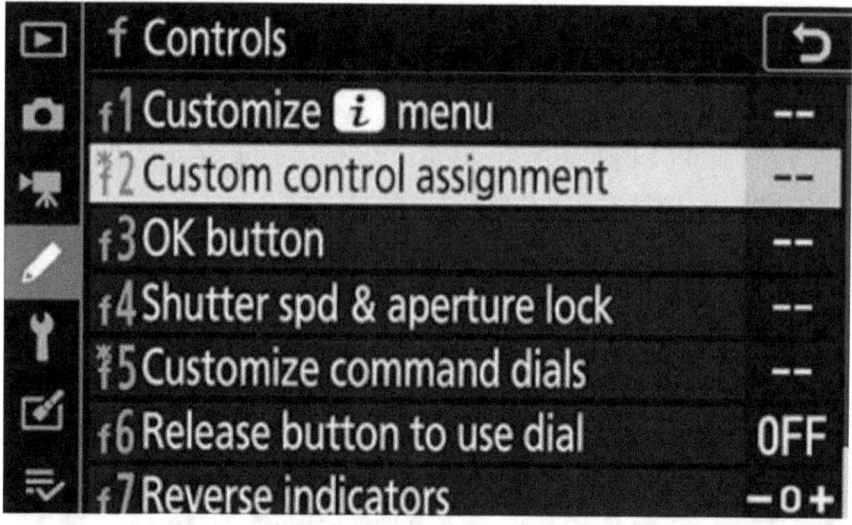

3. Choose a camera button that you want to assign to. For instance, click the Fn2 button and then the OK button.

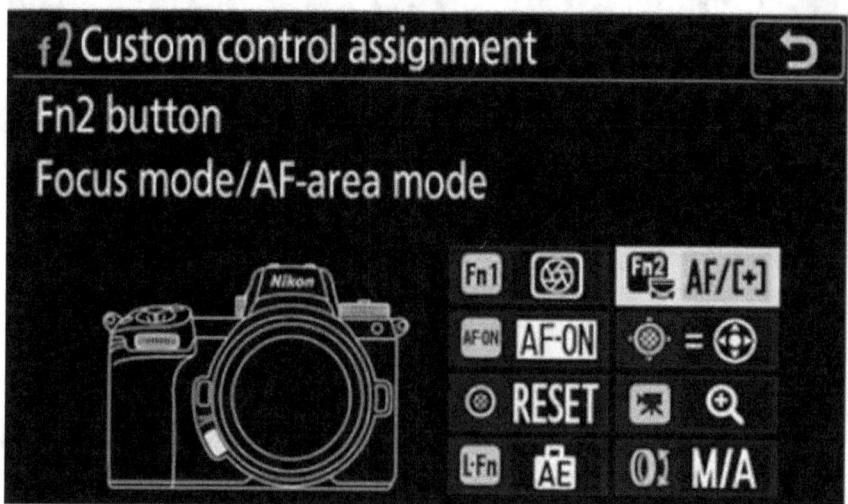

4. To assign the focus mode or area mode, click AF/[+] Focus mode and click the OK button.

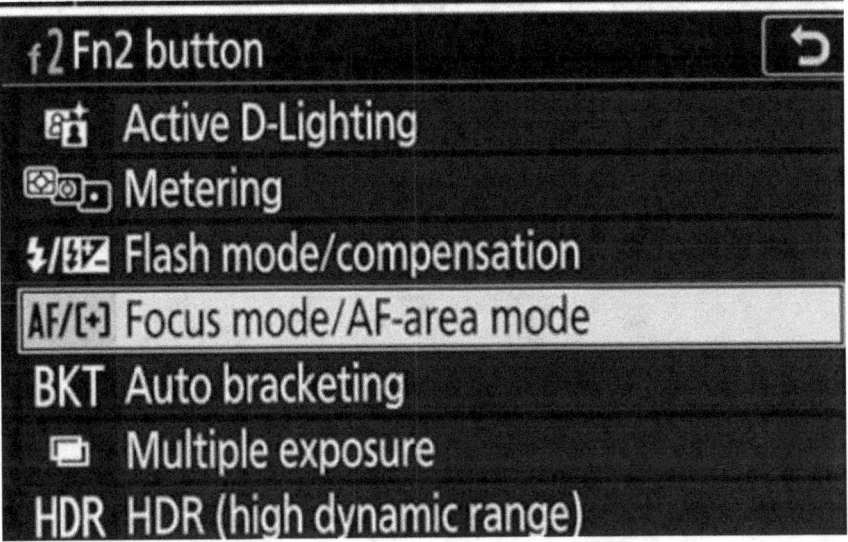

You can now access the Focus and AF-area modes at any time by using the button that you designated to focus mode/AF-area mode. Let us now examine how to access the Focus and AF-area modes using the Fn2 button that we recently assigned.

To choose a Focus mode with the camera external controls, follow these steps:

1. Press and hold the button you assigned in the aforementioned steps, or the Fn2 button on the front of the camera.

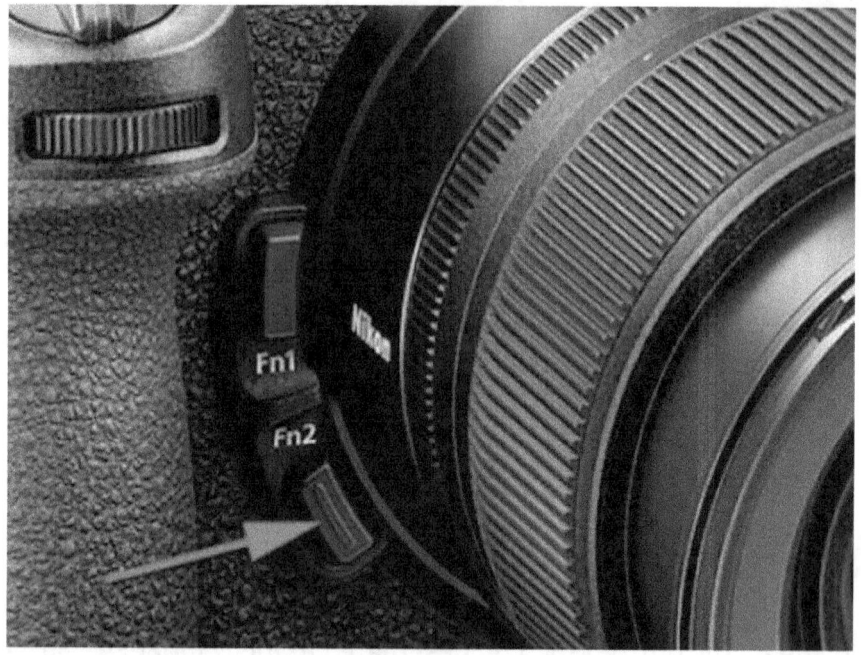

2. Rotate the main command dial located on the camera's back.

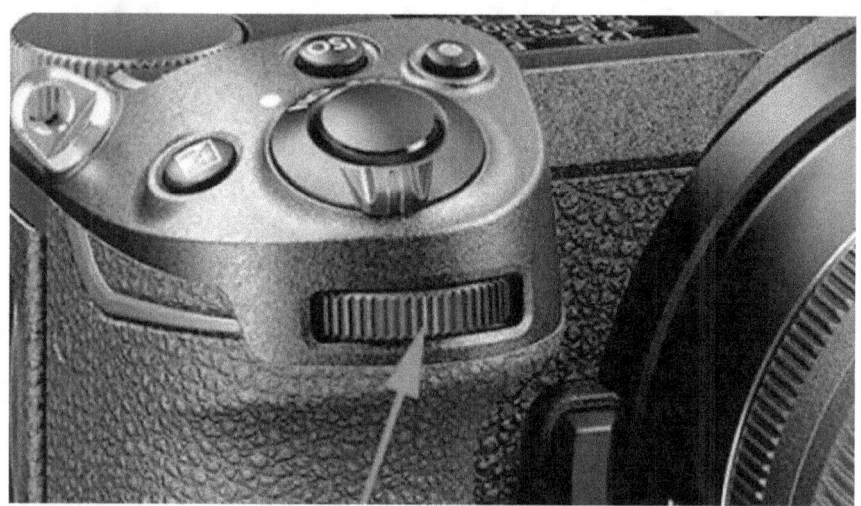

The symbols for the Focus mode will be shown at the top of the monitor or EVF.

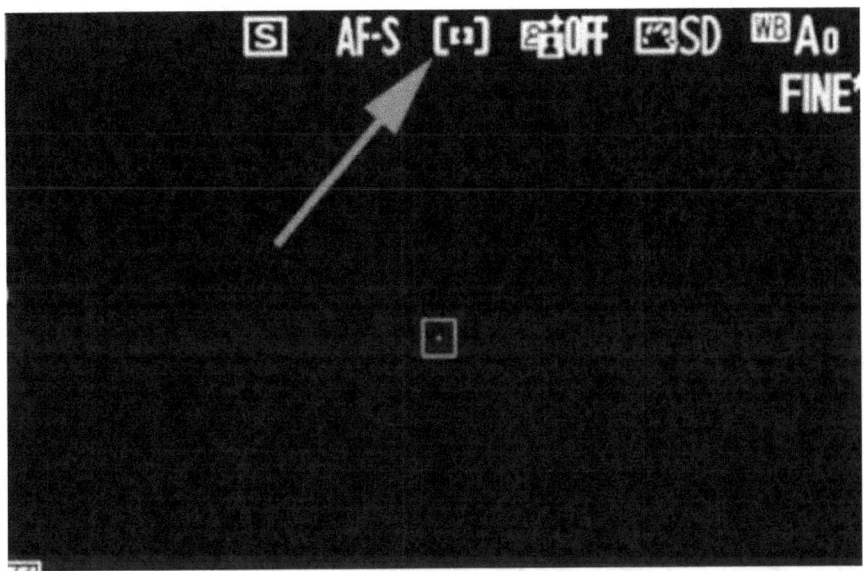

You can adjust the Focus mode by rotating the Main command dial on the back. Release the Fn2 button and cease rotating the Main command dial after the desired Focus mode appears on the screen.

Access the Focus and Autofocus from the Photo and Movie Shooting Menus

To choose an AF-Area and a Focus mode from the camera's Photo Shooting Menu, use these steps:

- Selecting a focus mode for still photography via the Photo Shooting Menu

1. Scroll to the right and choose Focus mode via the Photo Shooting Menu.

PHOTO SHOOTING MENU

Diffraction compensation	ON
Auto distortion control	ON
Flicker reduction shooting	OFF
Metering	▣
Flash control	--
Flash mode	⚡◉
Flash compensation	0. 0
Focus mode	AF-S

2. To choose a Focus mode, highlight it and touch or hit the OK button.

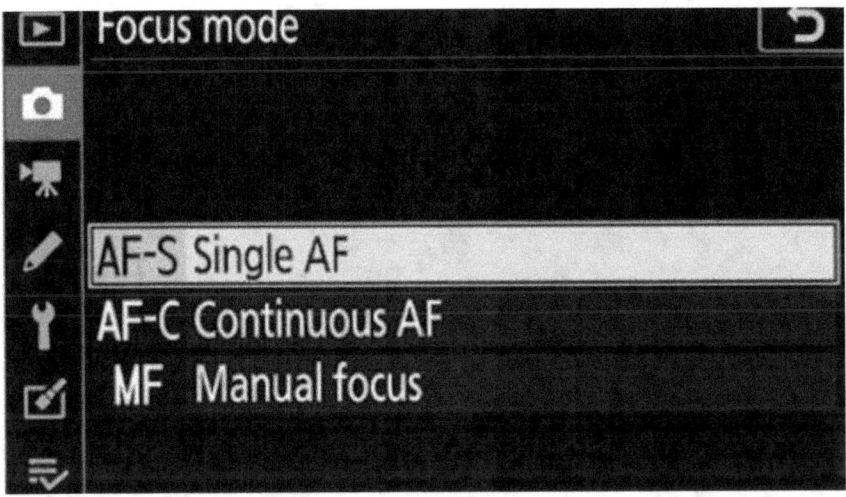

3. Scroll to the right and pick AF-area mode via the Photo Shooting Menu.

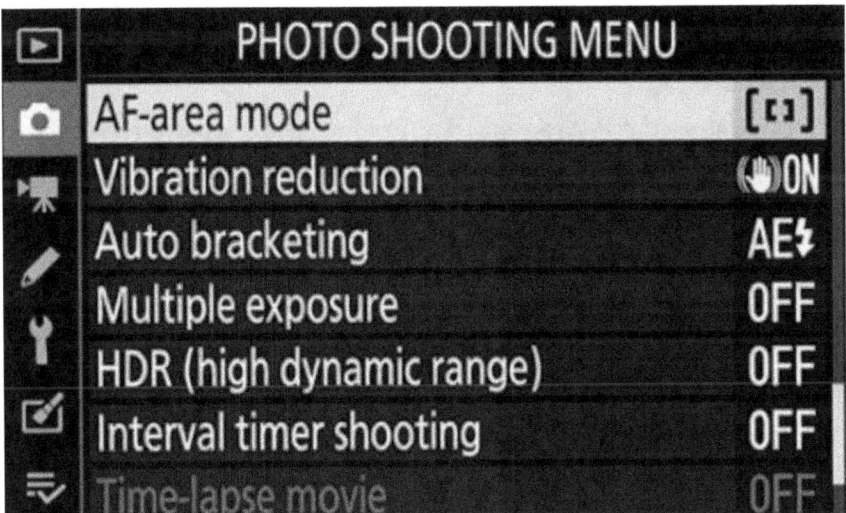

4. To pick an AF-area mode, highlight it and touch or push the OK button. Note; it is only in AF-S (Single AF) Focus mode is Pinpoint AF AF-area mode accessible. Also the AF-C

(Continuous AF) Focus mode is the only mode where the dynamic area AF AF-area mode is accessible.

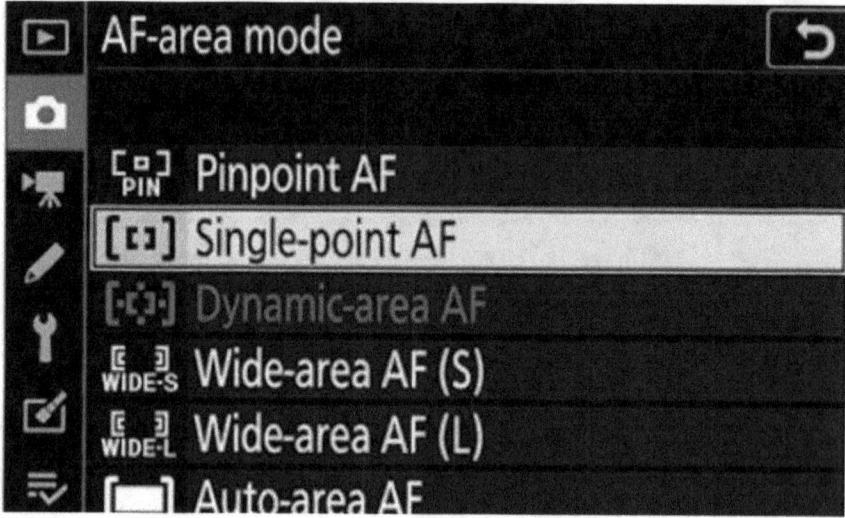

- Making Use of the Movie Shooting Menu

To choose an AF-Area and a Focus mode from the Movie Shooting Menu of the camera, follow these steps:

1. Scroll to the right and choose Focus mode from the Movie Shooting Menu.

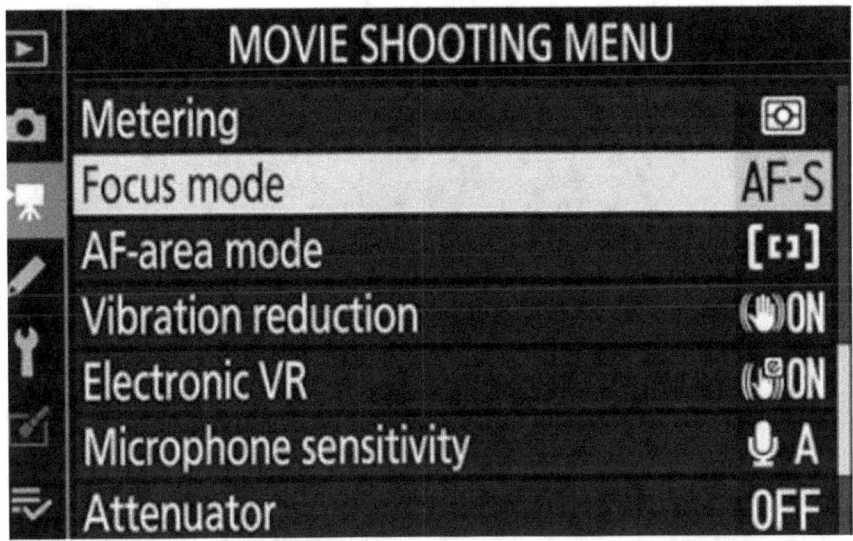

2. To choose a Focus mode, highlight it and touch or hit the OK button.

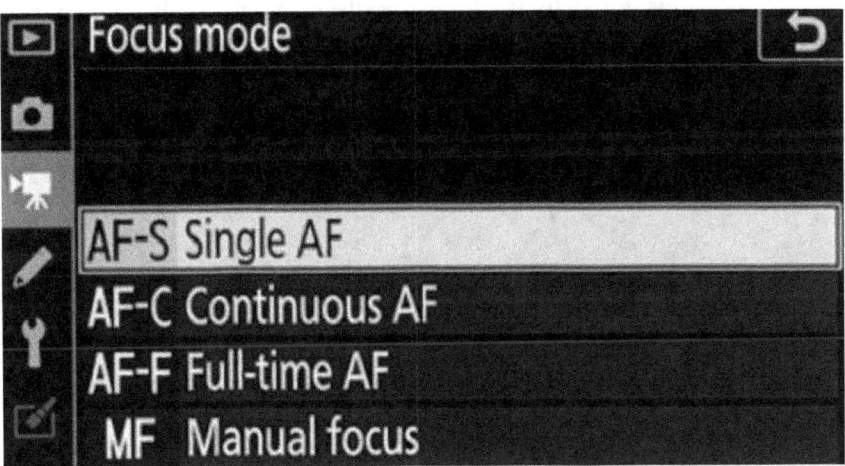

Let us now talk about how to use the Movie Shooting Menu to access the AF-area modes.

3. Scroll to the right and choose AF-area mode from the Movie Shooting Menu.

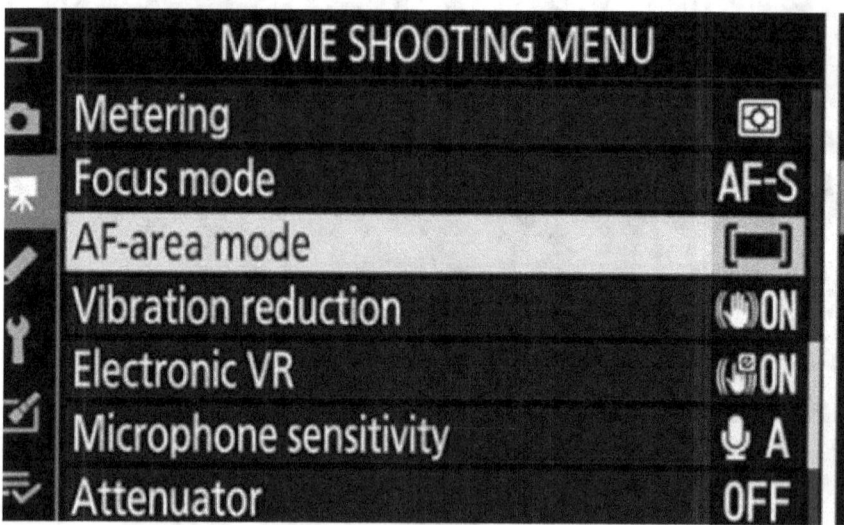

4. To pick your desired mode, click on it, or choose one of the various AF-area options and push the OK button.

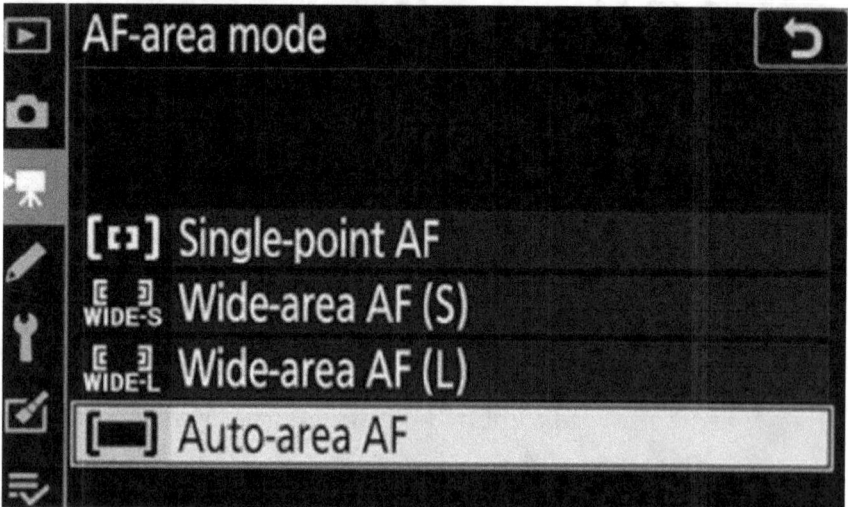

Note: When the Manual focus (MF) Focus mode is selected, the AF-area modes are turned off, grayed out, and inaccessible on the menus of the camera. When in MF mode, the camera assumes that you will be manually focusing and that you would use a tool such as focus Peaking to assist you in achieving sharp focus.

Single AF (AF-S)

The greatest use case for the Single AF (AF-S) mode is a stationary subject, such as shooting a building or landscape.

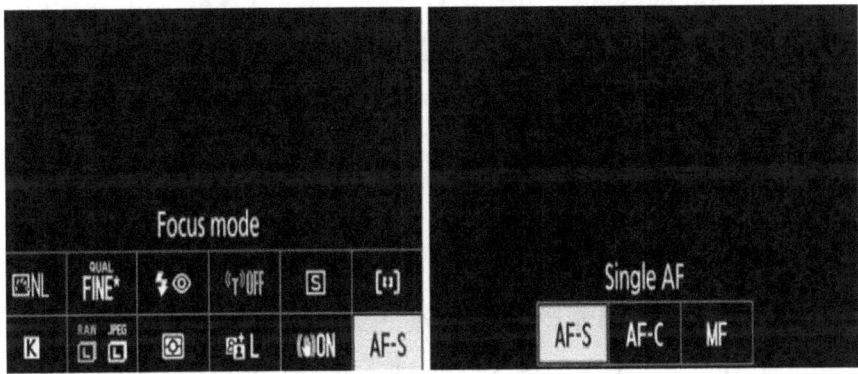

If you would like, you can utilize AF-S on slowly moving subjects, but you have to be cautious to change autofocus as the subject moves. When to employ this mode is explained in the following two scenarios:

1. The subject is in a fixed position: Pressing the Shutter-release button halfway down or completely down on the AF-ON button causes the AF module to rapidly lock focus on your subject and hold it there until you push the

shutter. The focus will become outdated and ineffective if your subject moves and you do not release and apply pressure on the Shutter-release button (also known as the AF-ON button) to refocus. Once your subject is in focus, snap a short photo using the camera. For subjects that are fixed or move extremely slowly under certain situations, this mode is ideal.

2. The Subject is constantly moving: You will need to put in a little more effort to do this. Because the autofocus mechanism latches on to your topic, it may lose focus if it moves even a little. To focus again, you will need to take your finger from the shutter-release button and push it again halfway down (or press the AF-ON button all the way down). To maintain precise focus if the subject moves, you will need to continuously release and push the Shutter-release button (also known as the AF-ON button) halfway down. In situations when your subject moves constantly, unpredictably, or just momentarily pauses, AF-S is usually not the ideal option to employ. In this instance, AF-C is preferable since it never locks focus and allows the camera to more effectively compensate for the movement of your subject to maintain focus.

Continuous AF (AF-C)

Maintaining focus while holding the shutter-release button halfway down or the AF-ON button completely down is referred to as the Continuous AF (AF-C) mode.

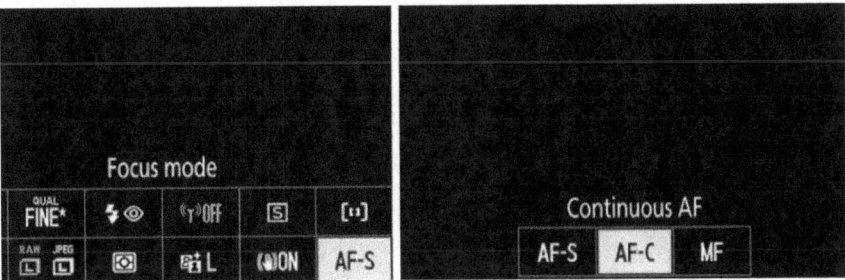

The following situations illustrate when and how to utilize this mode:

1. The subject is in a fixed position: Continuous-servo AF functions similarly to Single-servo AF while the subject is still, with the distinction that the focus never locks. The autofocus stepper motor will slightly alter the focus point if your subject or camera moves. You must exercise caution to avoid unintentionally moving the current autofocus point(s) off the subject, since the focus may decide to concentrate on background objects in this mode because the focus has not been locked.

2. The subject is constantly changing its position in the viewfinder: You must maintain your AF point on your subject in all AF-area settings whether it moves in the Viewfinder from left to right, right to left, or up and down. The AF point's size can be adjusted from tiny to huge.

3. The subject is either approaching or moving far from the camera: Another automated feature of the camera activates whether your subject is approaching you or

95

going away from you. It calculates the subject's path in milliseconds before the shutter firing, and is referred to as Predictive Focus Tracking. Predictive focus tracking shifts the lens elements slightly to match the subject's position when the shutter fires a few milliseconds after you fully depress the shutter-release button. To put it another way, while a subject is approaching you, the lens focuses a little bit ahead of them so that the camera has enough time to open the shutter blades and expose the image sensor just as the subject approaches the optimal focus point.

Full-Time AF (AF-F)

This mode is only efficient in Movie mode. Without your interference, this mode is intended to automatically maintain sharp focus on a recognized subject (i.e., Shutter-release or AF-ON). This mode offers autofocus that is updated continuously and is controlled by the AF-area mode that you have chosen. The AF-area mode you have chosen affects the focus square's (AF point's) dimensions and shape. To achieve correct focus in all AF-area modes except Auto-area AF, you must maintain the focus square (AF point) on your subject. In order to have the camera follow the subject and maintain focus while continuously updating focus, many videographers combine Auto-area AF mode with AF-F mode.

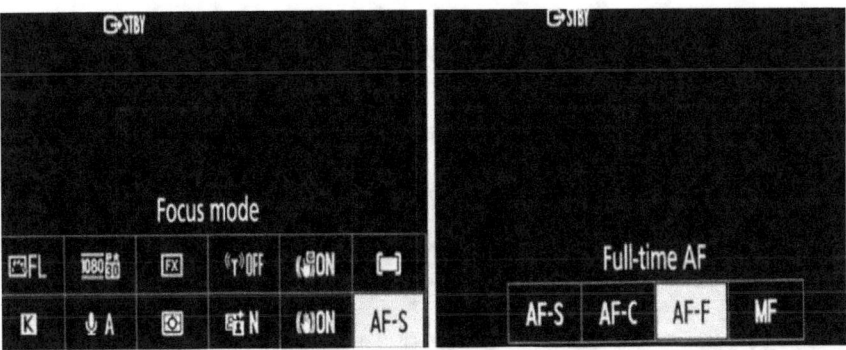

Unless you push the Shutter-release button halfway down or the AF-ON button entirely down, the camera does not lock focus while using the AF-F Focus mode. Instead, the focus updates continually when the button is held down. The shutter-release or AF-ON button may be released to unlock the focus and immediately return the camera to continuous autofocus. Put another way, the camera seems to be in AF-S mode while the shutter release button is pressed, and AF-C mode when the button is released. The only reason why you have to press the AF-ON or shutter-release buttons is to achieve a refocus. But most of the time, the camera will automatically keep focusing on your subject. Once again, the main task for using the AF-F Focus mode is to maintain your subject's focus, unless you are in Auto-area AF AF-area mode, in which case the camera follows your subject automatically.

Manual Focus (MF)

By rotating the focus ring on the lens, you can completely control the focus when the manual focus (MF) mode is engaged.

To apply focus, you can utilize your eyes or several focus aides for assistance.

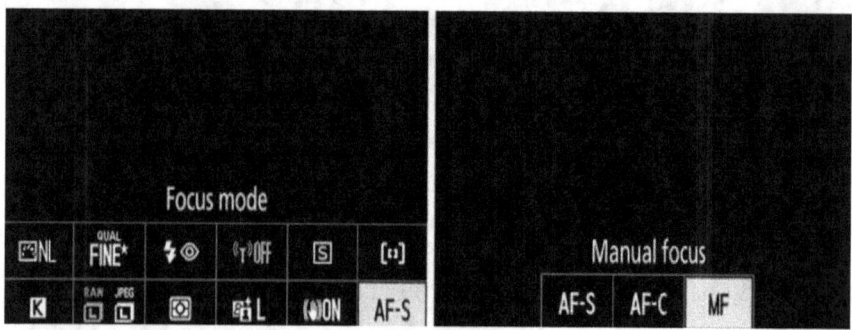

Let us look at how to enable and disable some features while using the MF mode.

- Activating or deactivating the manual focus AF point via the on screen

To activate or deactivate the manual focus (MF) mode's onscreen AF point, perform these steps:

1. To access the Manual Mode screen, go to Custom Setting Menu > an Autofocus > a10 Focus point settings > Manual focus mode.

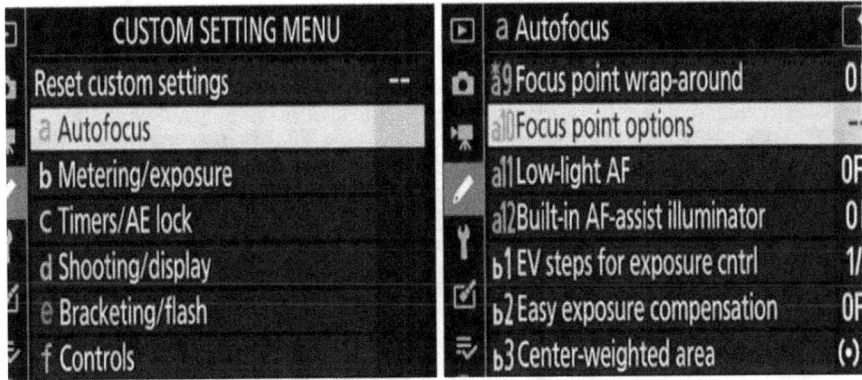

2. Select On to make the onscreen AF point active or Off to make it inactive.

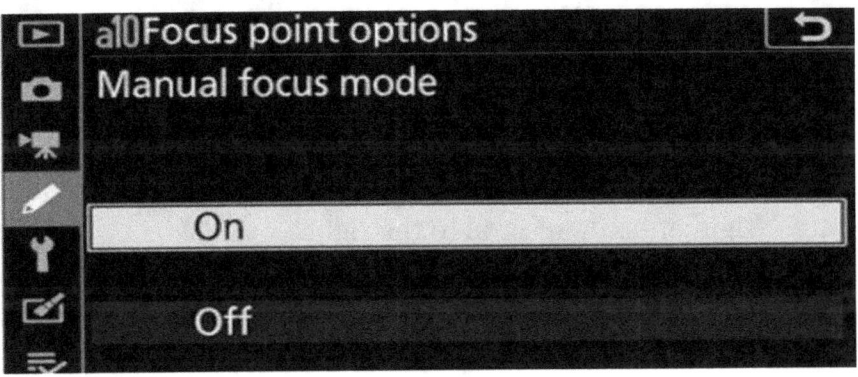

- Focus Peaking Highlights

You can utilize the capability known as "focus peaking" or "peaking highlights" to assist you in determining the ideal Manual focus. With the use of this function, you can precisely determine where the optimum focus is on your subject by having one of four colors around its boundaries. To choose a Peaking level and activate focus peaking, use the following steps:

1. From the Custom Setting Menu, choose Shooting/display and move the cursor to the right.

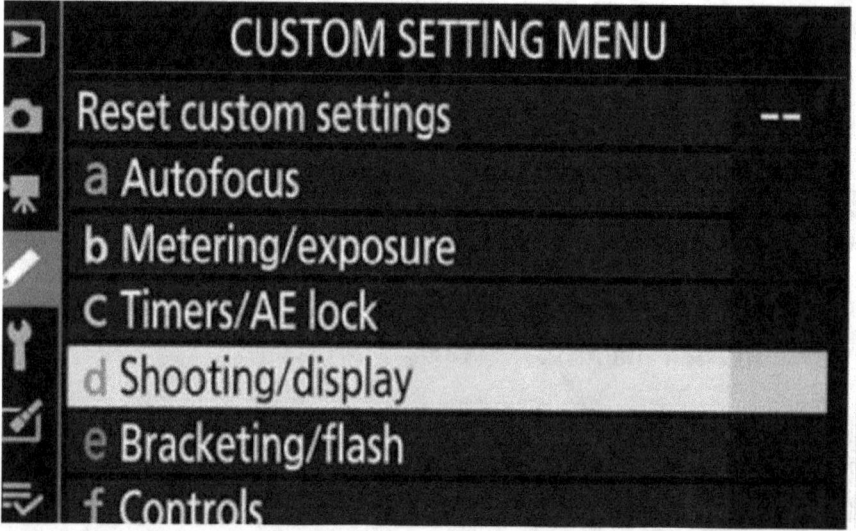

2. From the d Shooting/display menu, choose d10 Peaking highlights, then scroll to the right.

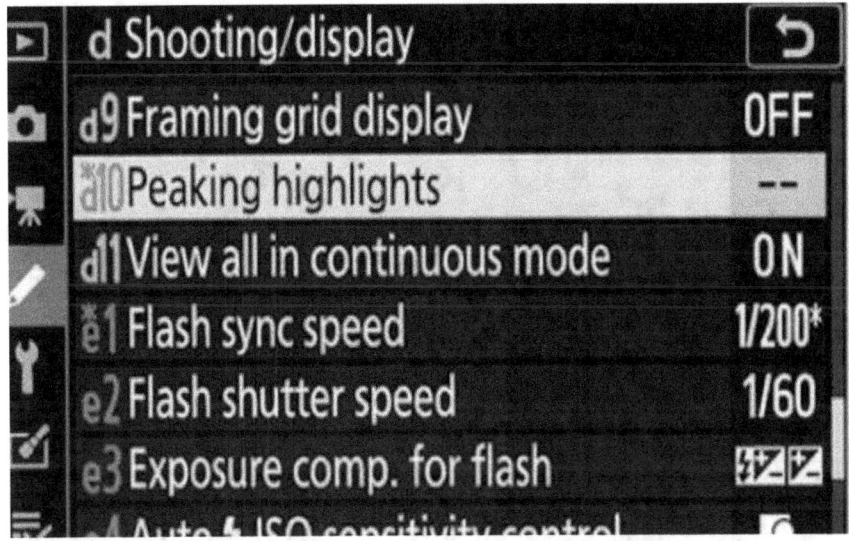

3. Select Peaking level and navigate rightwards

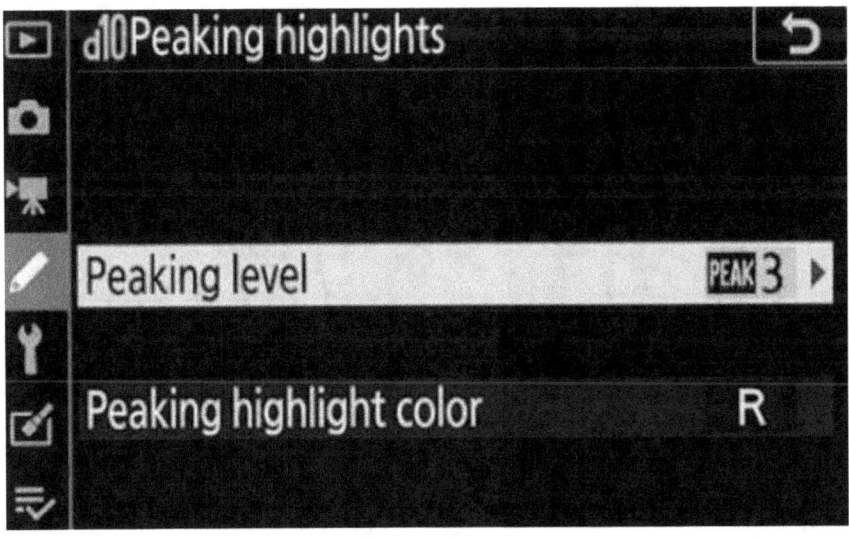

4. From PEAK 3 (high sensitivity) to PEAK 1 (low sensitivity), choose a peaking level. In order to lock in the sensitivity and intensity level, press the OK button or touch the selection. The

sensitivity and focus peaking highlight fringe will increase with increasing Peaking level number.

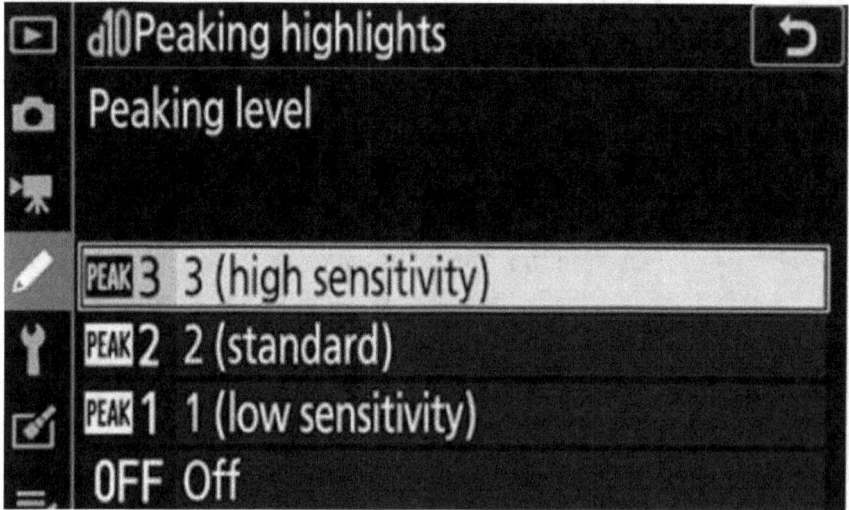

5. Scroll to the right and choose Peaking highlight color.

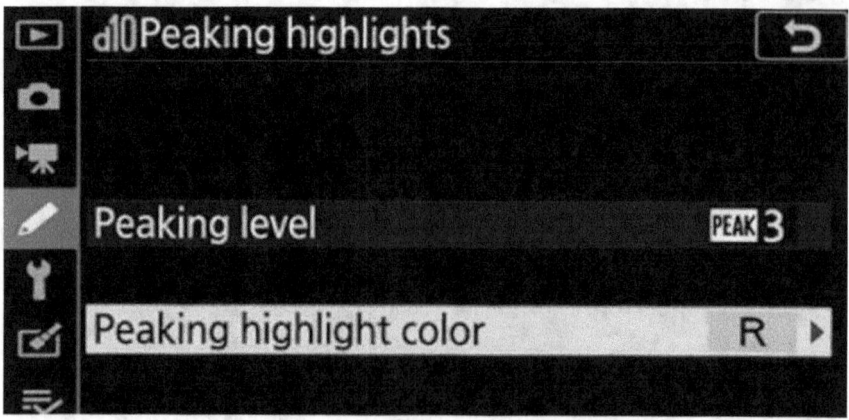

6. Select a highlight color from the following: white, blue, yellow, or red. To lock in your selection, hit the option or press the OK button.

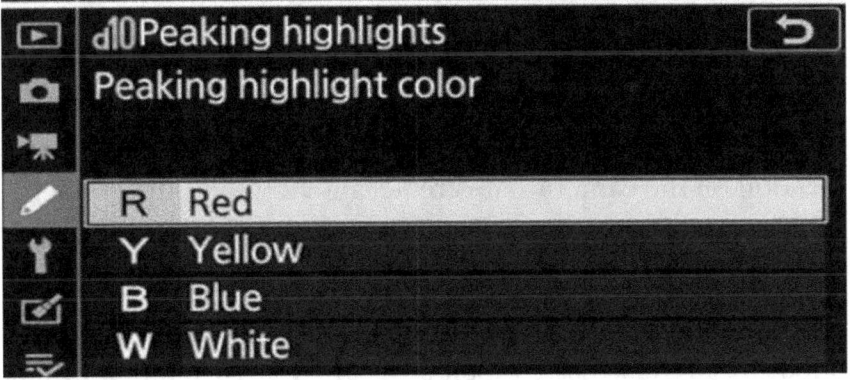

THE AF-AREA MODES

The purpose of the AF-area modes is to provide you flexibility over the size of the AF point, which indicates the current focus location on the camera. The greater the AF point, the greater is the region of the subject that is considered sharply focused. Press the i button to open the i Menu. To access the modes, you can also utilize a designated button or the Photo and Movie Shooting Menus. Let us look at each AF-area mode and talk about its functions.

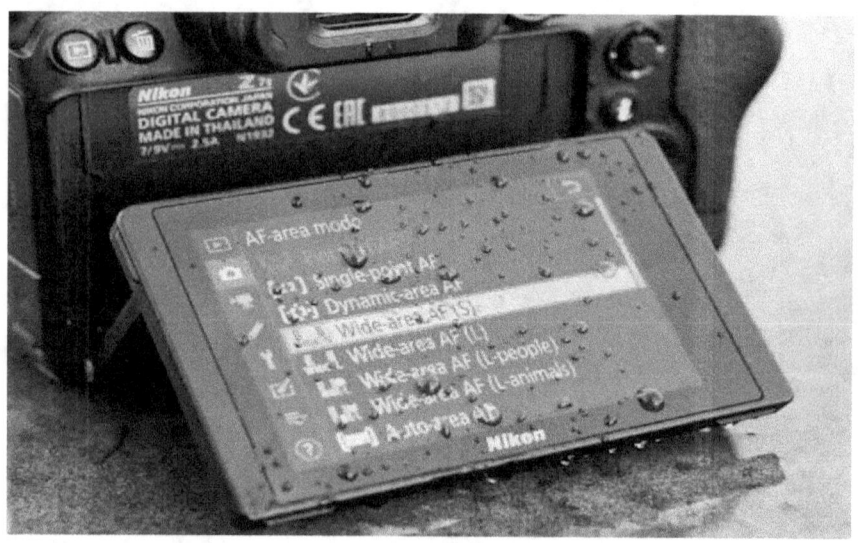

Pinpoint AF

You can choose a very narrow portion of your subject to focus on, with this option. You can, for example, shift the AF point to a leaf's water droplet or the pupil of an eye. It is designed to provide you with accurate autofocus so you can concentrate on certain regions. This mode only employs contrast-detection

(CDAF) autofocus, which is more accurate but requires more time to focus than phase-detection (PDAF) autofocus. Using the Sub-selector joystick or Multi selector pad, the Pinpoint AF square may be moved about within the 493 AF points on the Monitor or in the EVF. The Pinpoint AF square becomes green when the camera has a satisfactory level of focus.

Note: You can only use the Single AF (AF-S) Focus mode in order to access the Pinpoint AF AF-area mode. If the camera is in Continuous AF mode (AF-C), it is not accessible on the i Menu and is grayed out on the Photo Shooting Menu. Furthermore take notice that Movie mode does not support Pinpoint AF.

Single-point AF

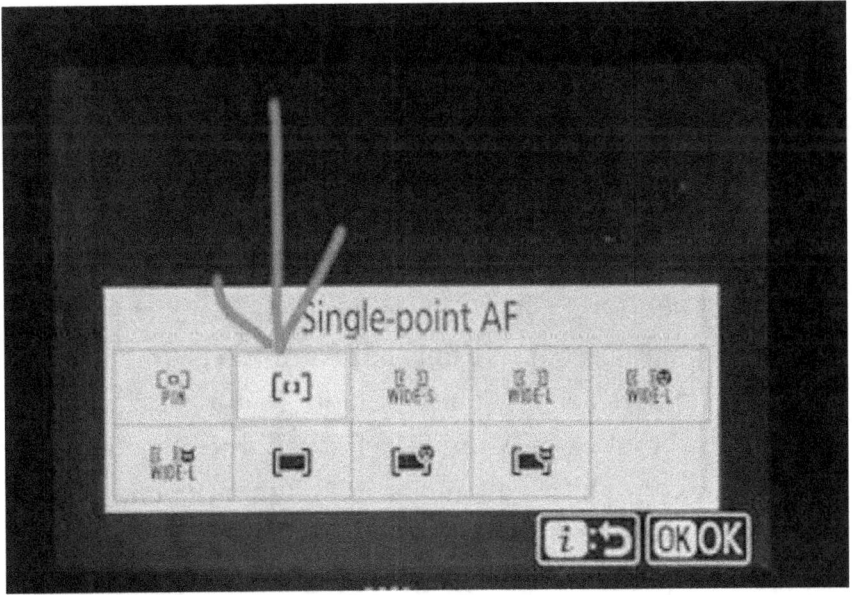

For many photographers, the ideal option is single-point autofocus. Compared to the Pinpoint AF frame, its AF point frame is bigger. Compared to Pinpoint AF, Single-point AF is quicker and still enables exact focus placement among the 493 AF points in the frame. According to Nikon, this mode starts with PDAF and ends with CDAF for focus verification. Using the Sub-selector joystick or Multi selector pad, the Single-point AF square can be moved about within the 493 AF points on the Monitor or in the EVF. If you are utilizing the Single AF (AF-S) Focus mode, the square will turn green after the camera has reached proper focus. The AF square will remain red while using Continuous AF (AF-C) Focus mode since this focus mode does not stop the camera from actively seeking focus. Both AF-S and AF-C Focus modes include single-point AF AF-area mode. Additionally, it can be accessed in the Photo and Movie modes.

Dynamic-area AF

Similar to Single-point AF, the Dynamic-area AF employs a central active AF point, but it also surrounds it with eight extra high-alert locations. One of the surrounding AF points can re-capture the subject if you or the subject moves and the current center AF point loses it. Within the red AF point frame, every single AF point is actively attempting to find focus. Using the Sub-selector joystick or Multi selector pad, the Dynamic-area AF frame may be shifted about within the 493 AF points on the Monitor or in the EVF. When focus is obtained, the frame does not turn green; instead, it remains red since all of the AF points are always trying to find focus.

It is only possible to use dynamic-area AF in Photo mode and not in Movie mode. When the camera is in Single AF (AF-S) Focus mode, you cannot use this AF-area mode. Dynamic-area AF will not be accessible on the i Menu and will be grayed out on the Photo Shooting Menu until you utilize Continuous AF (AF-C) Focus mode.

Wide-area AF (S)

With the exception of having a larger collection of AF points in each frame, this mode functions similarly to Single-point AF. The Single-point AF frame is much smaller than the Wide-area AF (S) frame. Within the red focus box, every unseen focus point is active. Using the Multi selector pad or Sub-selector joystick, the Wide-area AF (S) frame can be moved about within the 493 AF points on the Monitor or in the EVF. When utilizing Single AF (AF-S) Focus mode, the frame will become green when the camera has obtained proper focus. The camera will continue to seek active focus when in Continuous AF (AF-C) Focus mode, which is why the frame will remain red. Both the AF-S and AF-C Focus modes are available for the Wide-area AF (S) AF-area option. This option can be applied in both photo and movie modes.

Wide-area AF (L)

The only difference between this mode and Wide-area AF (S) is the size of the group of AF points inside its frame; otherwise, they operate similarly. All of the invisible focus points inside the red focus frame are active, and the Wide-area AF (L) frame is much bigger than the Wide-area AF (S) frame.

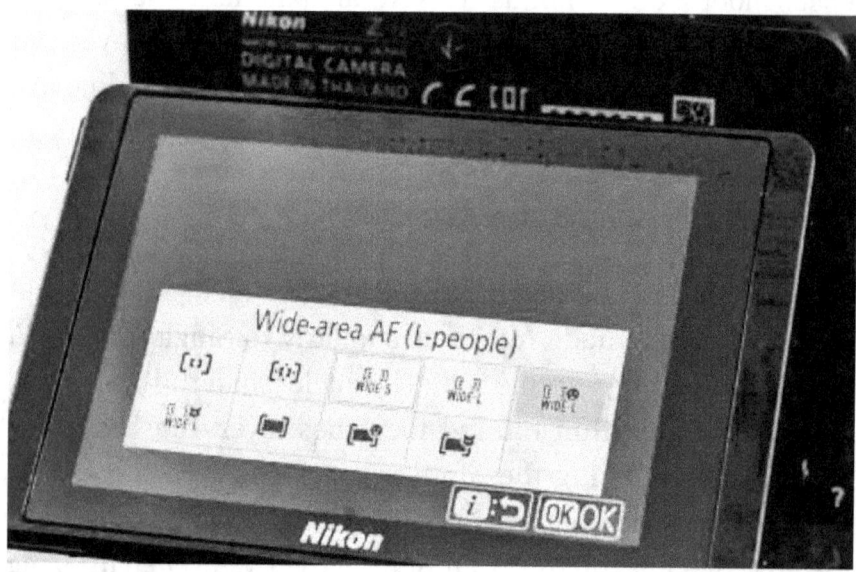

Using the Sub-selector joystick or Multi selector pad, the user may manipulate the AF point frame within the 493 AF points shown in the EVF or on the monitor. When utilizing Single AF (AF-S) Focus mode, the Wide-area AF (L) frame will become green to indicate that the camera has obtained proper focus. The camera will continue to seek active focus when in Continuous AF (AF-C) Focus mode, which is why the frame will remain red. Both AF-S and AF-C Focus modes are available for the Wide-area AF (L) AF-area mode. This option is accessible in the photo and movie modes.

Auto-area AF

The camera lets you choose which face to focus on when there are numerous faces in the picture while using this mode. It is evident that this option is a little more complicated than the other AF-area settings. When photographing human beings and using other Focus settings in addition to Auto-Area AF, the yellow focus frame will exhibit distinct behaviors.

1. When utilizing the AF-S Focus Mode: The camera will lock focus while you hold down the shutter-release button halfway or the AF-ON button all the way. The yellow focus frame will become green when the camera reaches proper focus. You have to press the shutter-release or AF-ON button one more time, in order to change the focus.

2. When utilizing the AF-C Focus Mode: The focus frame will constantly seek focus; hence, it will become red while you are holding down the shutter-release or AF-ON buttons, but neither green nor lock focus when good focus is achieved. You can cease pushing the Shutter-release or AF-ON button to stop the camera from changing the focus.

3. When in the AF-F Focus Mode (Movie): The yellow focus frame will move around a little bit as it continuously and automatically seeks focus. The camera makes every effort to maintain sharp focus even when your subject moves across the frame. You can hold down the AF-ON

button all the way or the shutter-release button halfway to lock the focus and make the yellow focus frame green. When you let go of the button, the focus updates on its own automatically.

With auto-area AF, the camera has complete control over the AF system. Note, you can not manually move a focus point around the screen, in this mode. Maintaining your subject within the red frame markers around the screen's four corners is necessary for the focus to function. To get the optimal focus on your subject, the camera will choose a set of AF points inside the frame. A collection of green rectangles will be shown, indicating the regions the camera uses for focusing. Depending on the Focus Mode you have chosen, these non-person AF locations can signal excellent AF in a number of ways, much like the person-based Auto-area AF yellow focus frame:

1. When focusing in AF-S mode: The little green frames will show up anywhere within the red corner borders when you press the AF-ON or shutter-release buttons halfway down. Holding the button down locks the autofocus. You must remove pressure and then press the Shutter-release or AF-ON button one more to update focus.

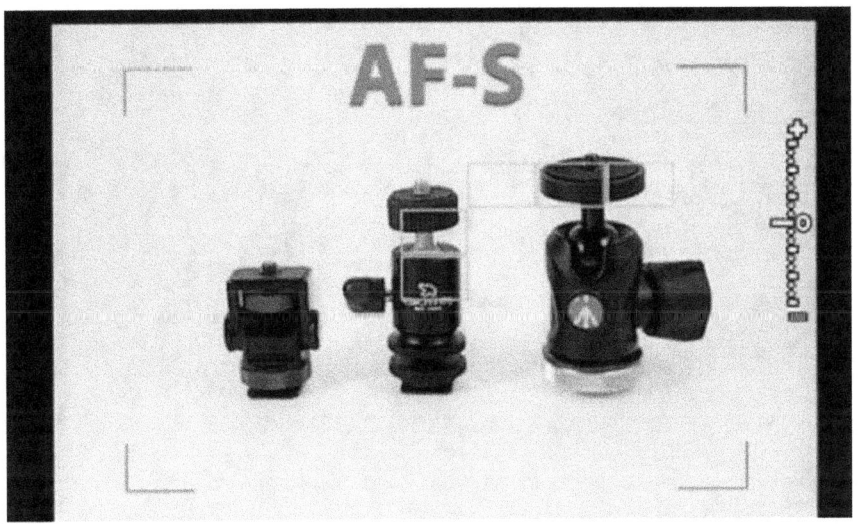

2. When using AF-C Focus Mode: Holding down the shutter-release or AF-ON button will cause a cluster of tiny red AF points to appear inside the red corner borders while you are using the AF-C Focus mode. Since the grouped AF points are always seeking focus, they will neither lock into focus nor glow green when excellent focus is obtained. The red AF point group will shift to show you how the autofocus is updating as it focuses on even the smallest movements from the camera or subject. If you remove your grip on the shutter release or AF-ON button, the Z7 ceases to update the focus.

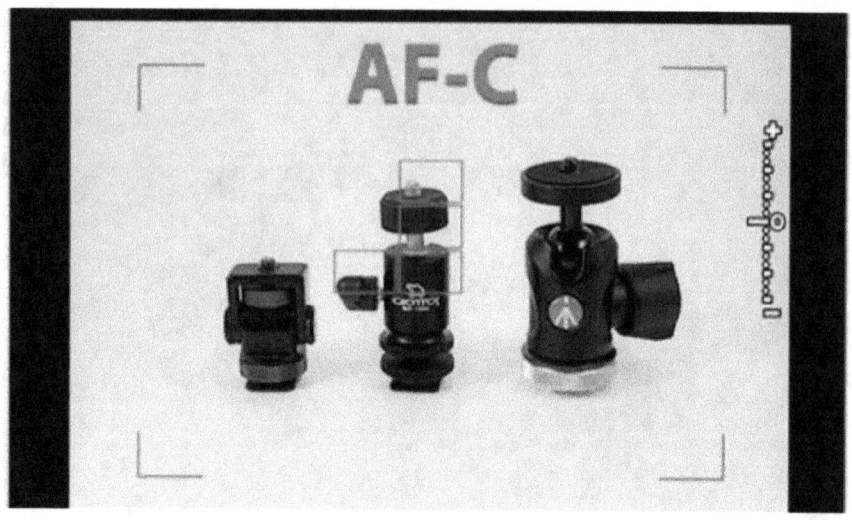

3. When using AF-F Focus mode: No AF points will show up within the red corner bounds when using the AF-F Focus mode. The camera will attempt to focus on your topic sharply as long as it stays within the corner bounds. A set of green AF points will appear and the focus will lock if you hold the Shutter-release button Partially down or the AF-ON button all the way down. Once there is nothing in the frame to indicate what is in focus, the camera updates focus automatically as soon as you let go of the button.

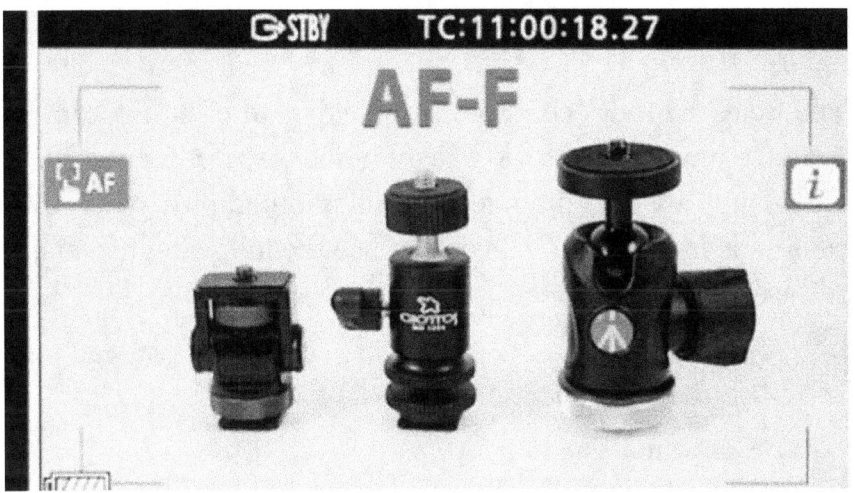

RELEASE MODES

The Release Modes control how quickly and often the camera can take images. Note; the release modes are not for recording video, they are only intended for still photography. When your camera is in Photo mode, you can use the following five major release modes:

1. "Single frame

2. Continuous L

3. Continuous H

4. Continuous H (extended)

5. Self-timer"

Nevertheless, there are two Release modes for Movie mode as well, which allows you to snap 16x9 low-res photos in Movie mode before or during a video recording session:

1. Single Frame

2. Continuous

Use the procedures listed below to choose a Release Mode:

1. Click the Release mode button.

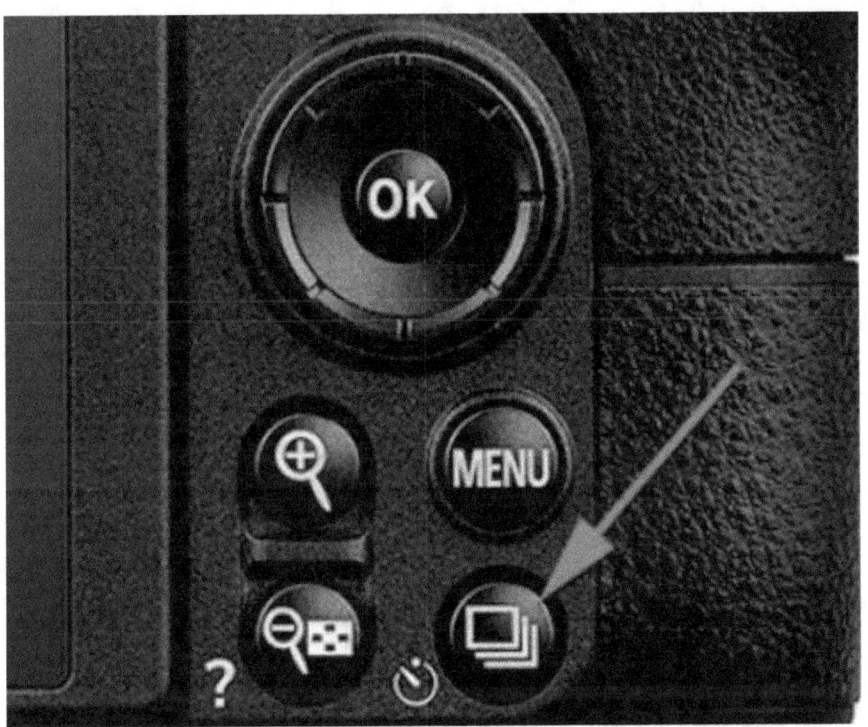

2. The selection screen for the Release mode will then appear.

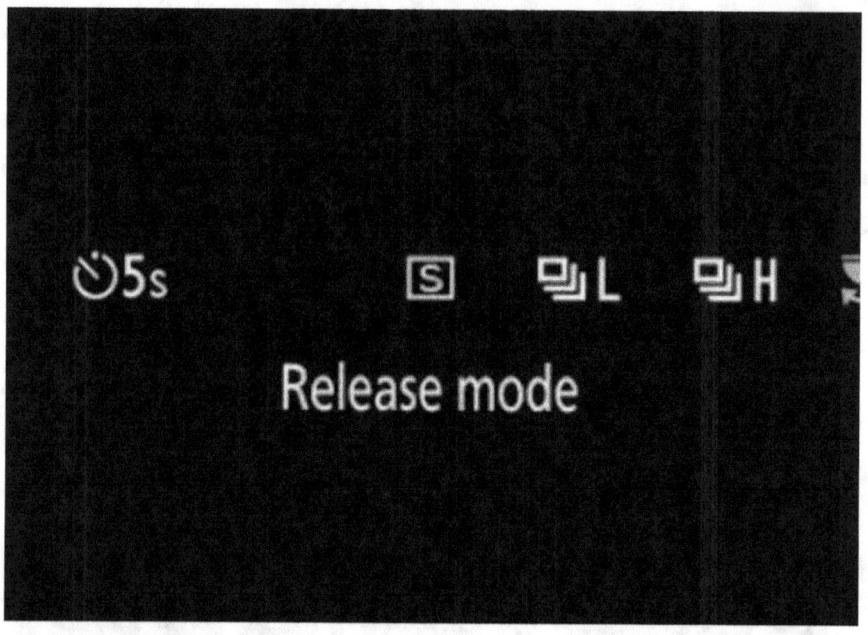

3. Press and hold the back Main command dial to choose the preferred Release Mode.

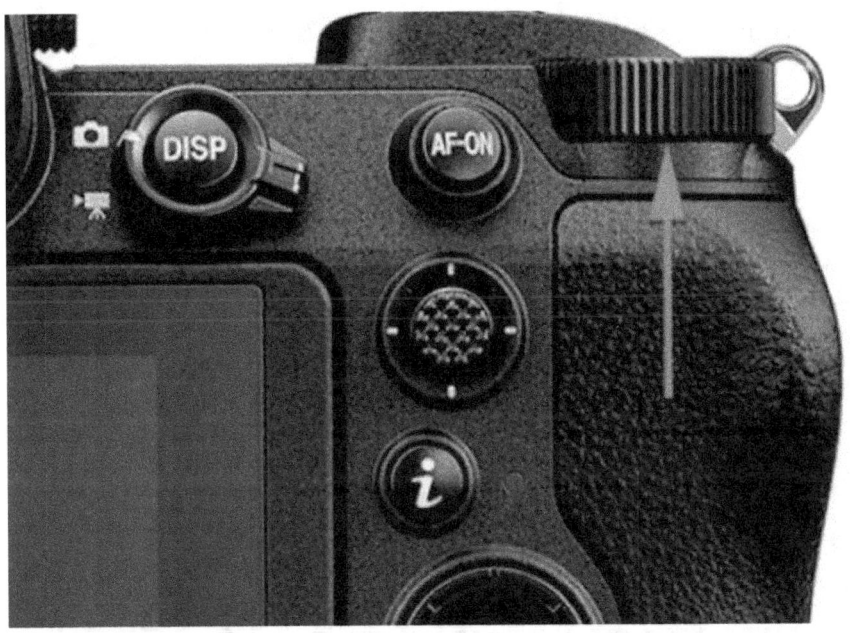

4. To modify any sub-settings, rotate the front Sub-command dial.

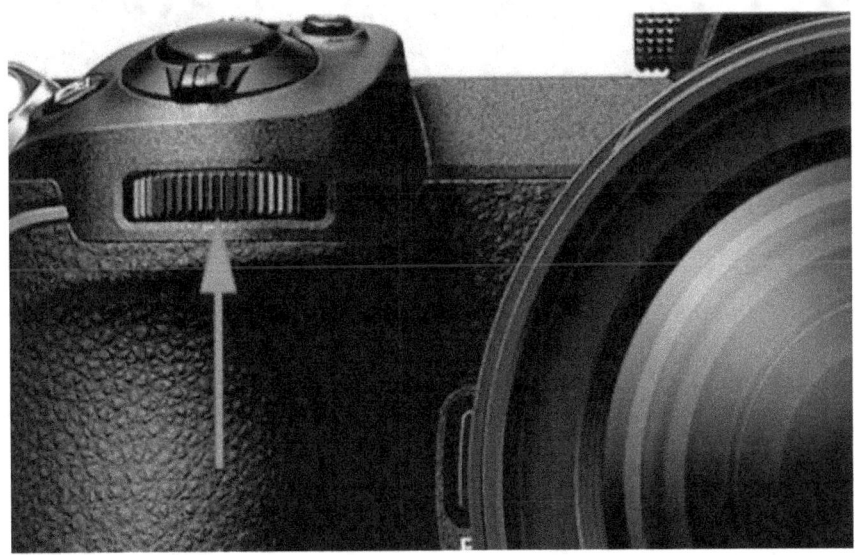

5. Ensure that the camera's Photo/Movie selection lever, which surrounds the DISP button, is in the proper position (Photo or Movie mode) before pressing the Release mode button to access the Release modes.

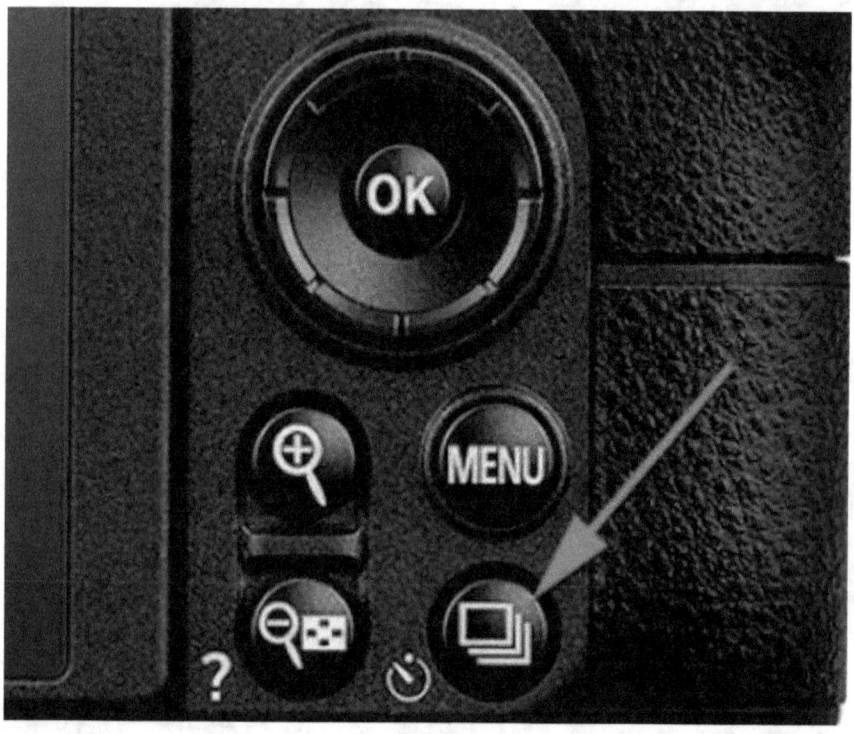

6. Observe the lower-left corner of the Control panel on top of the camera, to see the Release mode (such as S, L, H, or H*) that you have currently chosen, without having to access the settings on the camera.

The different Release Modes have been fully explained below;

Single Frame

This is the most basic release mode. Every time you completely press the shutter-release button in this mode, it only captures one image.

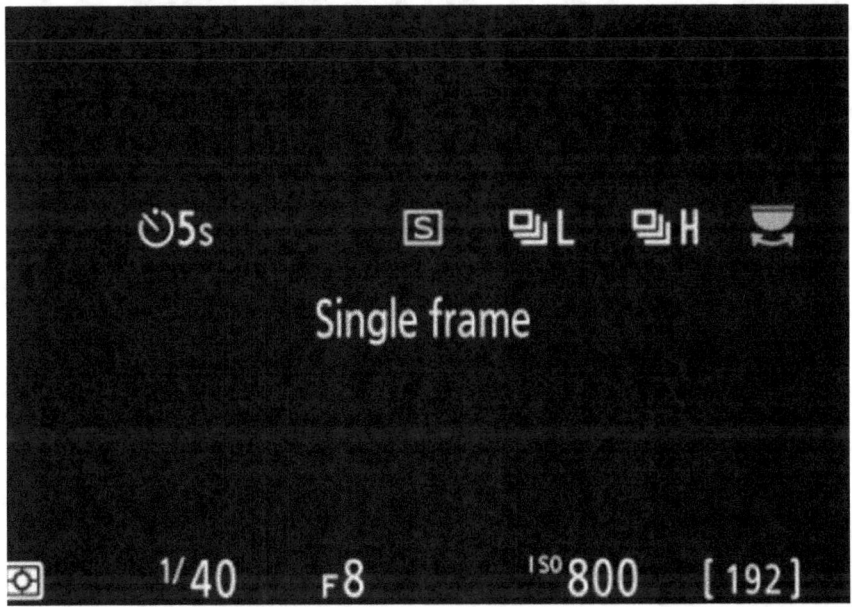

In the Photo mode, there are five accessible options; in the Movie mode, there are two available options, the first option of which is the Single frame (S). To choose the Single Release Mode, do the following actions:

1. Click on the Release mode button to bring up the Release mode interface.

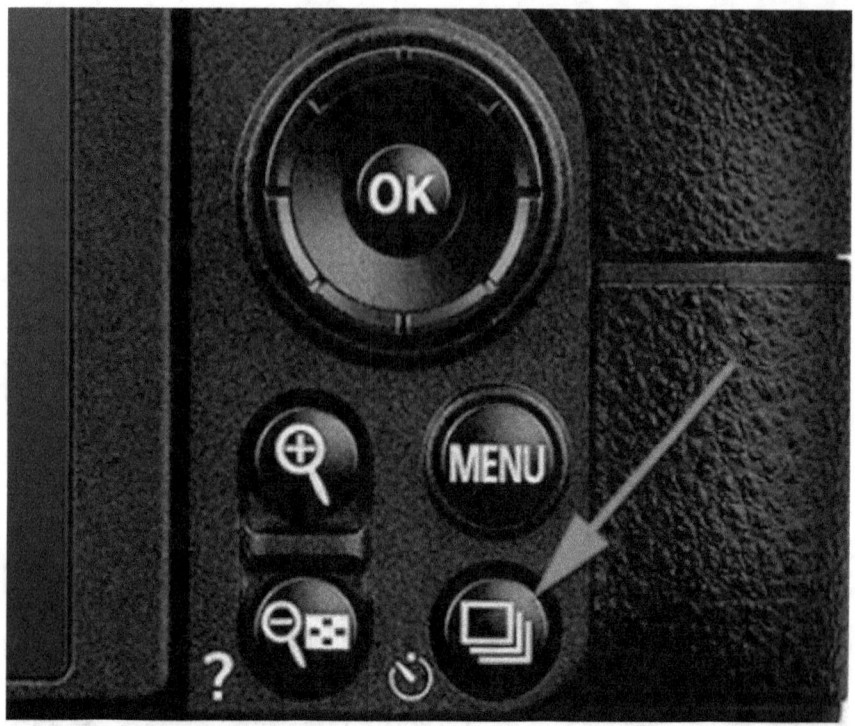

2. To lock in the mode, turn the rear Main command dial until Single frame is highlighted, then click the OK button.

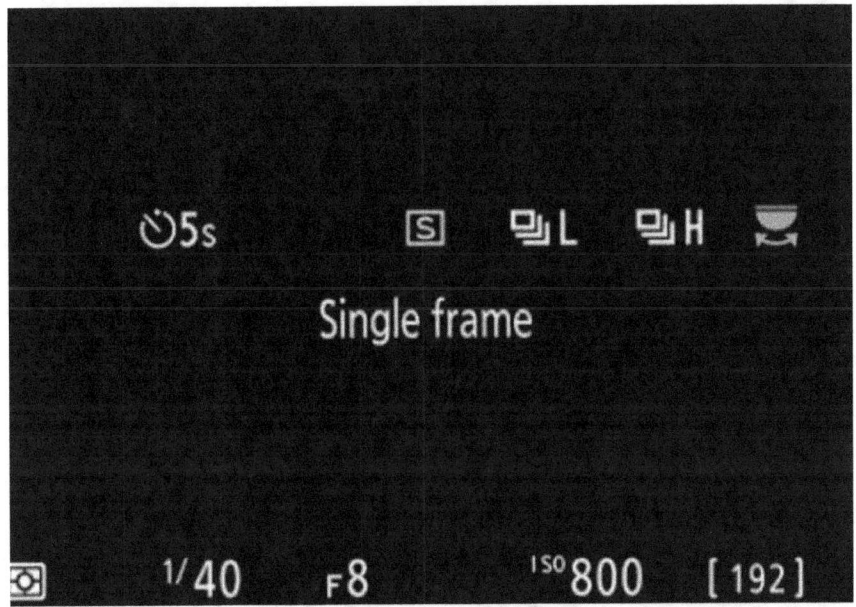

Note, however, that this mode lacks speed. This is for photographers using either the Photo or Movie modes, which allow them to take one 16x9 shot at a time. This setting is often used by nature photographers who are more focused on precise depth of field and outstanding composition than rapid speed. Since it only allows just one photo to be taken per shutter release button click, this mode is especially excellent for capturing portraits, graduations, weddings, and events.

Depending on the frame size and frame rate that are presently set for Movie mode, the camera can capture one 16x9 photo in Single Frame Release mode while it is in Movie mode. When you are not making a video, you can capture one image at a time in this mode. If you depress the Shutter-release button completely while filming, the camera will record one frame as a still image without interrupting or damaging the video that is now being recorded. Also, a maximum of 50 still images can be taken during each video recording.

Continuous (Movie mode only)

Only the Movie mode offers the Continuous Release feature. The Continuous L and Continuous H modes in Photo mode are not the same as this option. Holding the shutter-release button down for up to three seconds (3 s) enables you to snap a large number of 16x9 frames in a burst while you are not recording a video. You can only capture one 16x9 frame at a time when recording a video, with each click of the shutter-release button.

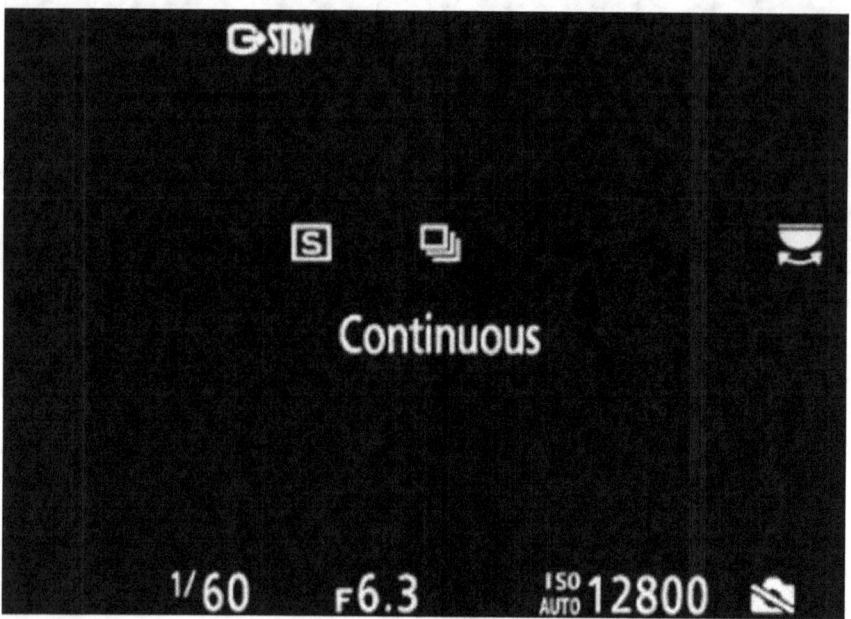

Use the instructions listed below to access the Continuous mode;

1. Ensure that the photo/movie selector lever is in the lower position and the camera is in the movie mode.

2. Click on the Release mode button to bring up the Release mode interface.

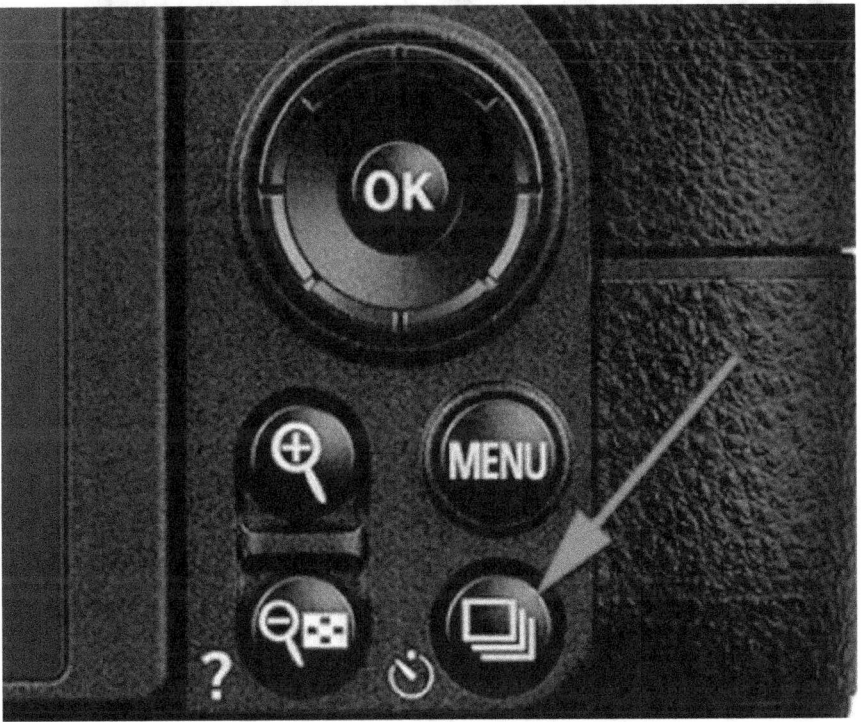

3. To lock in the mode, turn the rear Main command dial until Continuous is highlighted, then click the OK button.

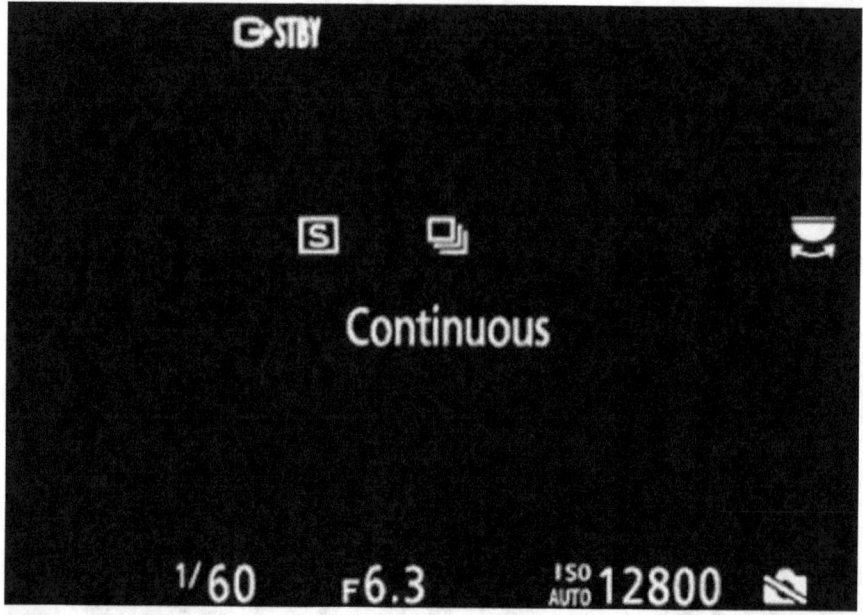

Note: Use the Continuous mode in the Movie mode (not the Continuous L or H in the Photo mode) with extreme caution. You can use Single frame (one photo at a time) or Continuous (many images in a burst) to snap pictures while you are not recording video. If you depress the shutter-release button, the camera will capture hundreds of 16x9 pictures using the quiet electronic shutter in a matter of seconds. When you use the Continuous mode without taking a video, it is essentially like taking a manual three-second movie, where every frame is stored on your camera's memory card as a single picture. These images are all the size of a single 16x9 video frame. A 1080p image is around 2 MP in size, but a 4K image is approximately 8 MP in size. You can shoot practically as many images as you want, or more than you thought you wanted, in spite of the camera's restricted buffer since the XQD card's transfer rate is so rapid that it almost quickly clears the buffer. The camera stops the capture after three seconds in an effort to restrict your large individual picture intake.

Conversely, if you have the Single frame or Continuous Release mode chosen and you push the Shutter-release button while recording a video, the camera will only take one 16x9 picture for each press of the shutter-release button; this will not interfere in any way with the video capture process.

Continuous L

You can choose a frame rate in Continuous L Release mode from one to five frames per second (fps). This option only works in the Photo Shooting Mode.

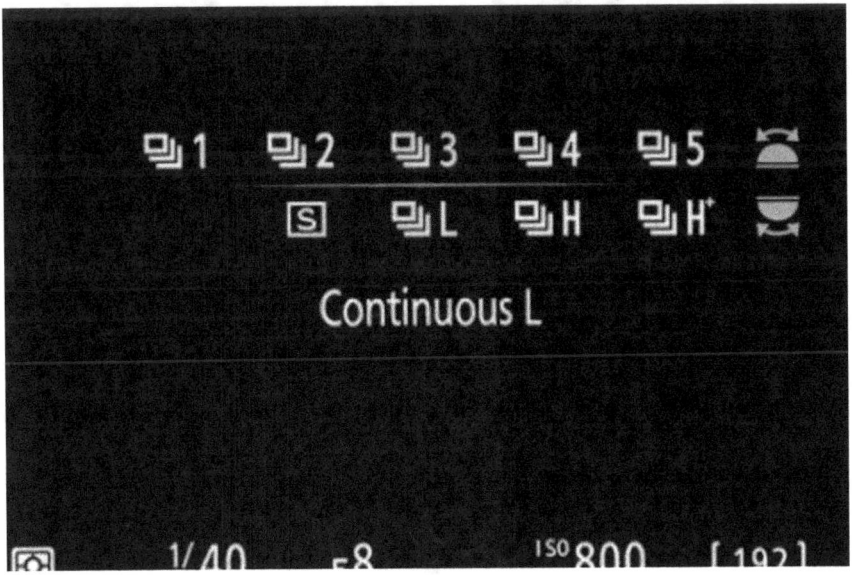

Use the instructions below to access the mode.

1. Click on the Release mode button to bring up the Release mode interface.

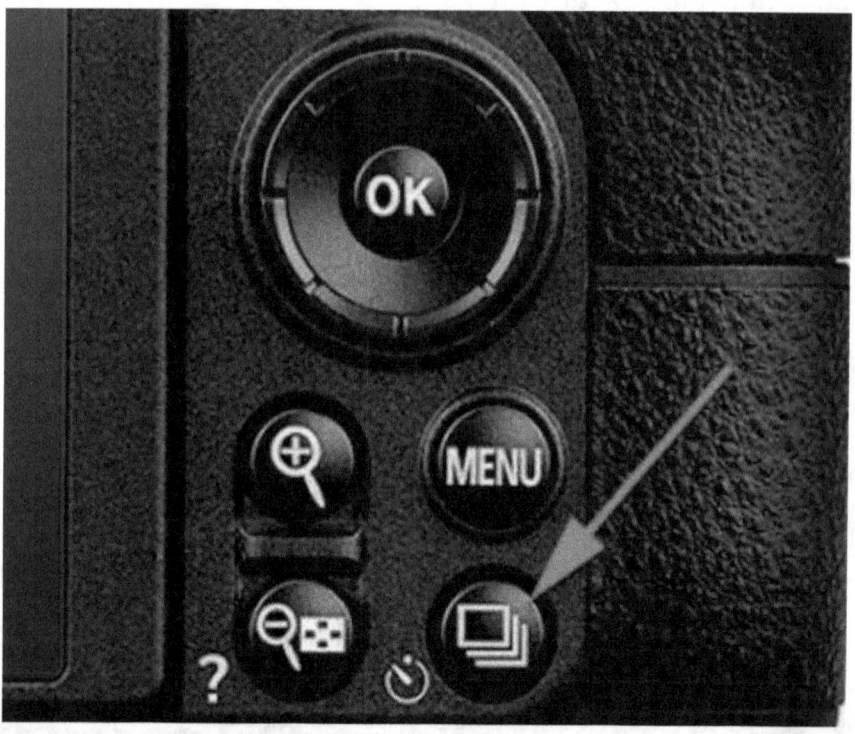

2. Next, rotate the rear Main command dial until the Continuous L symbol is visible.

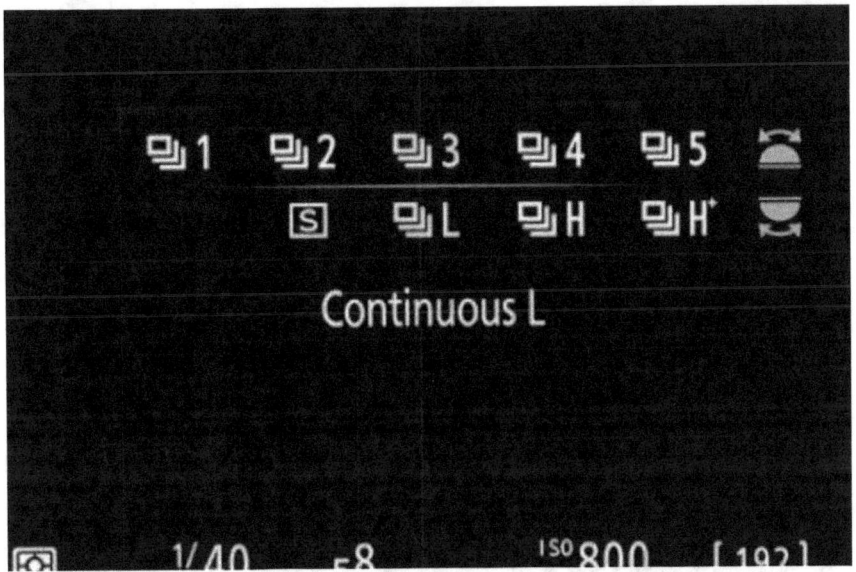

Now spin the front Sub-command dial and set a frames-per-second rate, from 1 to 5 fps, for snapping with the camera's mechanical shutter. In order to lock the mode, press the OK button.

The frame rate will decrease to a maximum of 4.5 fps for JPEG, TIFF, 12-bit NEF (RAW), or 12-bit NEF (RAW) + JPEG modes if you are shooting in Silent photography mode (Electronic shutter, page 307); the camera is limited to 3.5 fps in 14-bit NEF (RAW) mode.

When utilizing the mechanical shutter on your camera, there will be a temporary blackout of the EVF or Monitor during each photo capture. When shooting in this mode, the camera will give autofocus (AF) and auto exposure (AE) for each picture.

Continuous H

The purpose of this release mode is to capture images at the maximum frame rate that the camera is capable of handling. Keep in mind that Movie mode does not support this mode. To enter the mode, do the following actions:

1. Press the Release mode button to bring up the Release mode interface.

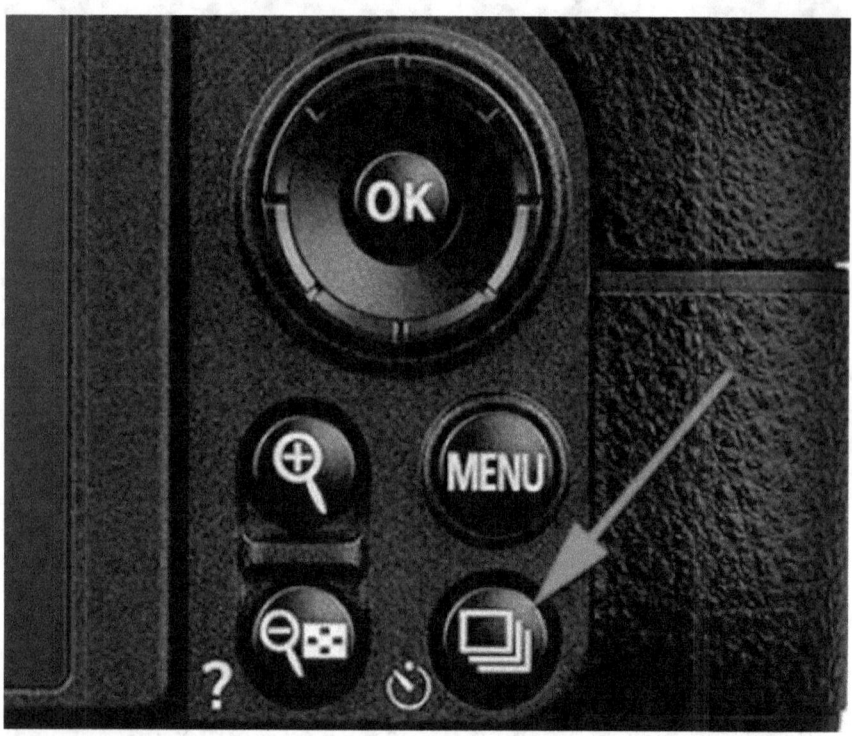

2. Next, rotate the rear Main command dial until the Continuous H symbol is visible. In order to lock the mode, press the OK button.

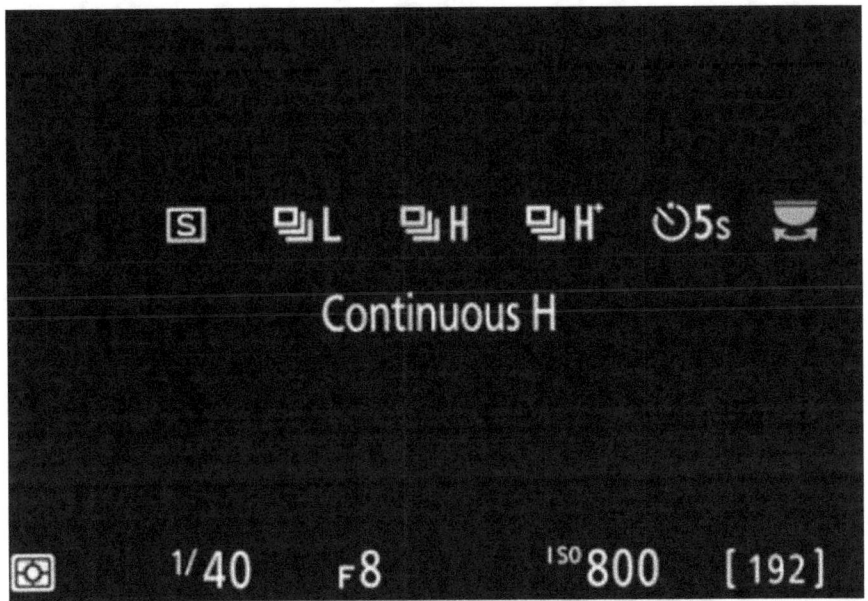

When using the camera's mechanical shutter in JPEG, TIFF, 12-bit NEF (RAW), or 12-bit NEF (RAW) plus JPEG modes, the typical frame rate is 5.5 frames per second. The camera can only capture images at a maximum frame rate of 5 frames per second when using the mechanical shutter in 14-bit NEF (RAW) or 14-bit NEF (RAW) + JPEG settings. When utilizing the mechanical shutter on your camera, there will be a temporary blackout of the EVF or Monitor during each photo capture.

The frame rate for JPEG, TIFF, 12-bit NEF (RAW), or 12-bit NEF (RAW) + JPEG modes will decrease to a maximum of 4.5 fps if you are using the Silent photography mode (Electronic shutter, page 357). In 14-bit NEF (RAW) or 14-bit NEF (RAW) + JPEG modes, you can only shoot at 3.5 frames per second.

129

When shooting in this mode, the camera will give autofocus (AF) and auto exposure (AE) for each picture.

Continuous H (Extended)

This mode operates at a high speed. The Continuous H (extended) Release mode does not have an EVF or monitor blackout while shooting at its maximum 9 frames per second. Keep in mind that Movie mode does not support this mode. Use these steps to get access to the mode:

1. Press the Release mode button to bring up the Release mode interface.

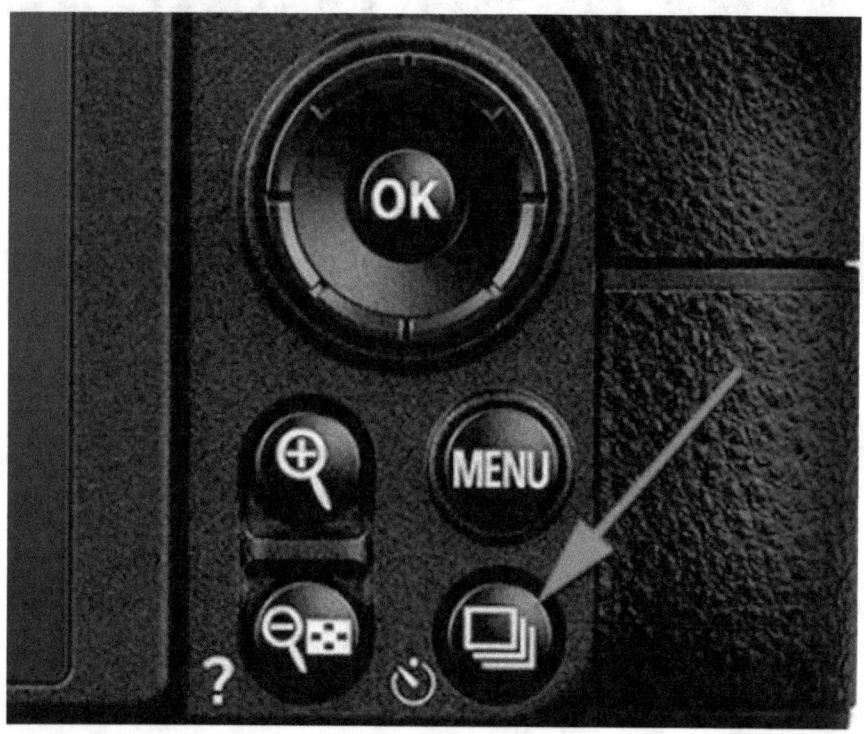

2. Next, rotate the rear Main command dial until the highlighted Continuous H (extended) appears. In order to lock the mode, press the OK button.

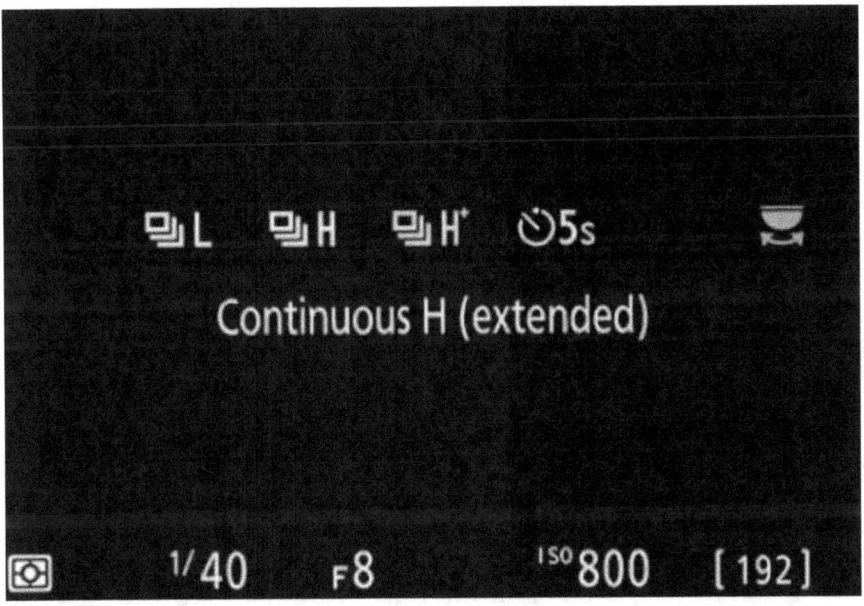

If you use this mode, be aware that the camera can only record in JPEG, TIFF, 12-bit NEF (RAW), or 12-bit NEF (RAW) plus JPEG formats at a maximum of 9 frames per second. The camera can only capture images at a frame rate of 8 frames per second with the mechanical shutter when using the 14-bit NEF (RAW) or 14-bit NEF (RAW) + JPEG settings.

The frame rate for JPEG, TIFF, 12-bit NEF (RAW), or 12-bit NEF (RAW) + JPEG modes will decrease to a maximum of 8 fps if you are shooting in Silent photography mode (Electronic shutter, page 357). In 14-bit NEF (RAW) or 14-bit NEF (RAW) + JPEG modes, you can only shoot at 6.5 frames per second. At nine frames per second, the camera will automatically focus. Note: The Z7 can only meter the first frame; however, for firmware versions lower than version 2.0, update your firmware since update 2.0 removes this restriction and now the camera will meter every frame. Note: When shooting in this mode, flicker reduction is not enabled.

Self-Timer

To set your camera to start taking images a few seconds after you hit the shutter release button, use the Self-timer Release mode. When you push the Shutter-release button halfway down, the camera will autofocus, and when you press it all the way down, the self-timer will begin. Keep in mind that Movie mode does not support this mode. To enter this mode, do the following actions:

1. Press the Release mode button to bring up the Release mode interface.

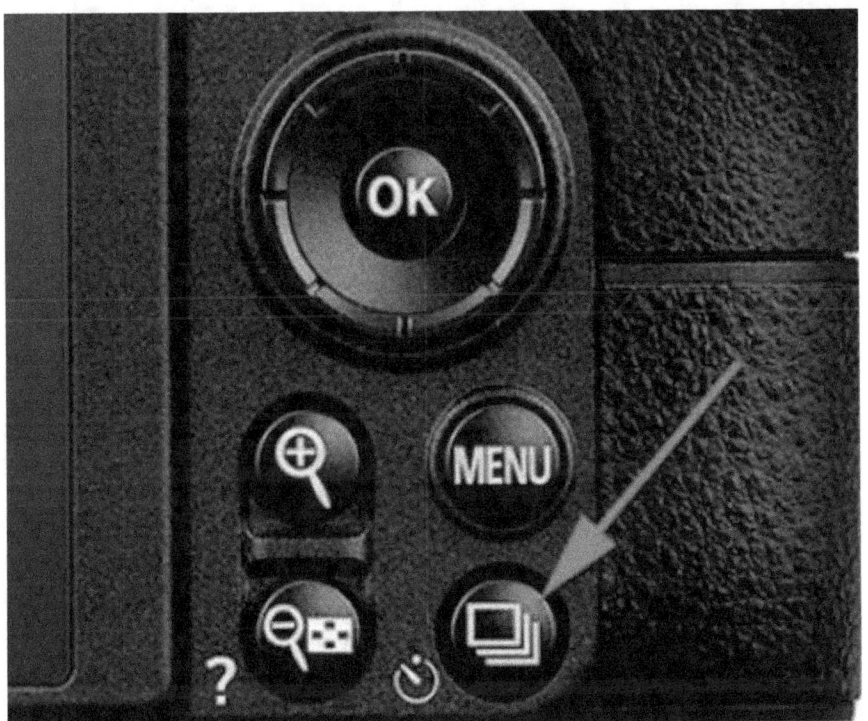

2. Next, rotate the rear Main command dial until the Self-timer icon appears.

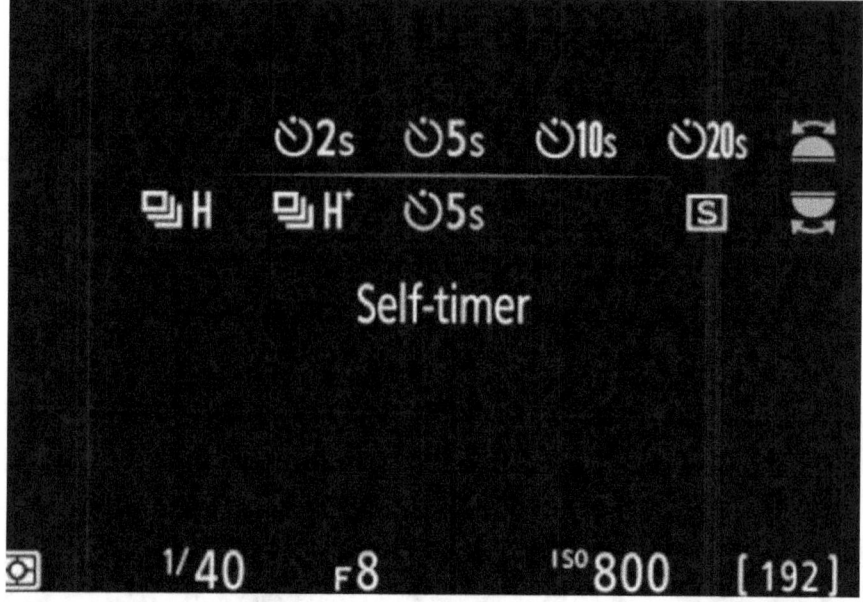

3. Turn the front Sub-command dial now, and choose between a 2 or 5 or 10 or 20-second delay timeout. In order to lock the mode, press the OK button. Note that; the Self-timer's factory default timeout is set to 10 seconds.

To change the timeout to 2, 5, 10, or 20 seconds, use Custom Setting Menu > c Timers/AE lock > c3 Self-timer. Additionally, you can adjust the interval between each shot (from 0.5 to 3 seconds) and the amount of shots (up to 9) that are taken during each self-timer cycle using the c2 Self-timer. You can adjust the beeping sound that occurs when the Self-timer counts down the seconds before the shutter opens by going to Setup Menu > Beep settings. When you activate the Self-timer mode by pressing the shutter-release button, the buzzer (if enabled) and the self-timer bulb will flash about twice a second.

The Self-timer bulb will turn on constantly and the beeping will double in pace as the final two seconds approach. When the beeping becomes more rapid, it means your time is almost up. The picture will be shot before the beeping timer stops. Lastly, should you want to end the self timer, all you have to do is hit the Playback or MENU button.

Touch Shutter Release and Autofocus (Tap Shooting)

With the Nikon Z7, you can touch your subject on the camera's display to start autofocusing or shoot shots. There are two components to tap shooting—Touch AF and Touch shutter/AF—that are offered by Nikon.

1. Touch Shutter/Auto Focus: The Z7 will lock autofocus while your finger is on the subject shown on the screen and will hold off on releasing the shutter until you remove it. The camera will snap a photo of the subject by automatically pressing the shutter, as soon as you raise your finger.

2. Touch AF: The camera will lock onto autofocus on the subject when your finger is placed on it, but it will not snap a picture. The camera will not refocus when in AF-F mode until you take your finger off the screen.

To enable either or both of the Tap shooting methods, follow these steps:

1. Tap the Touch shutter/AF icon that will be displayed on the screen.

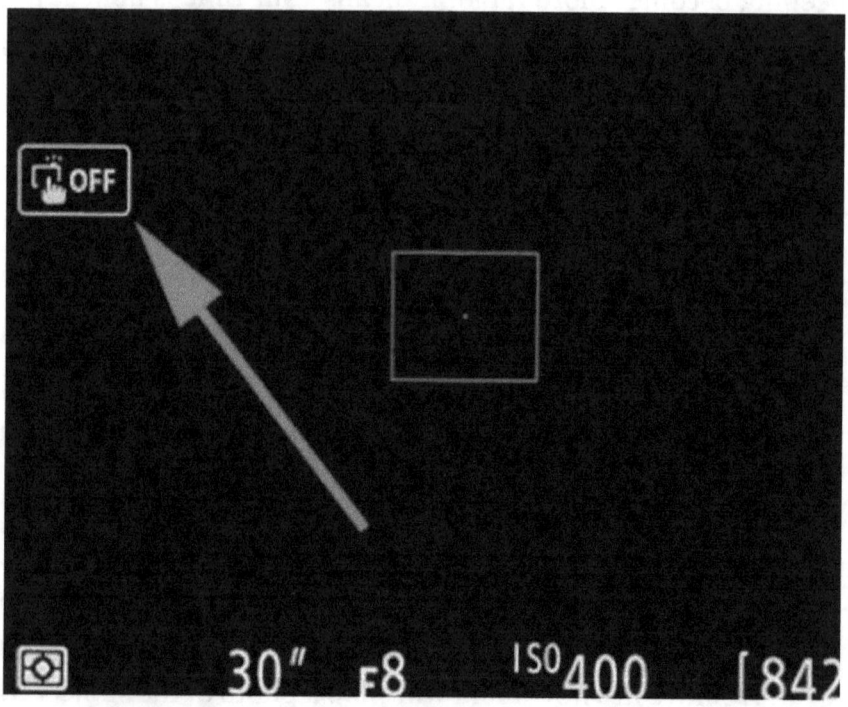

2. You will see a pop-up box that says "Touch Shutter/AF: On."

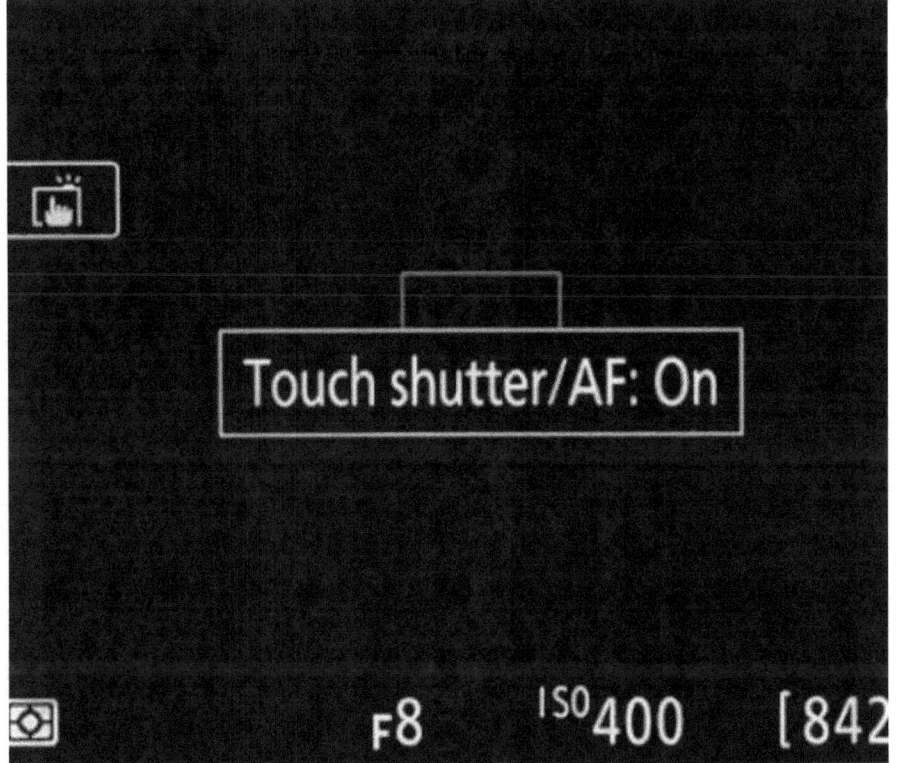

Touch shutter/AF: On

F8   ISO400   [842

3. At this moment, the OFF word would disappear from the symbol, allowing both the Touch shutter and Touch AF to become operational (Touch shutter/AF). You can use Tap shooting and quit the subsequent steps, if you want to use both Touch Autofocus and Touch Shutter Release.

4. The popup box with the words "Touch AF: On" will reappear when you click the Touch shutter/AF symbol once more.

The abbreviation AF which signifies that the autofocus is active, will be included in the symbol; this means only the "Touch AF" is active. Touching the monitor merely triggers focusing, because the touch shutter release is deactivated. You can skip to the next step if you wish to use the standard shutter-release button to capture images and touch

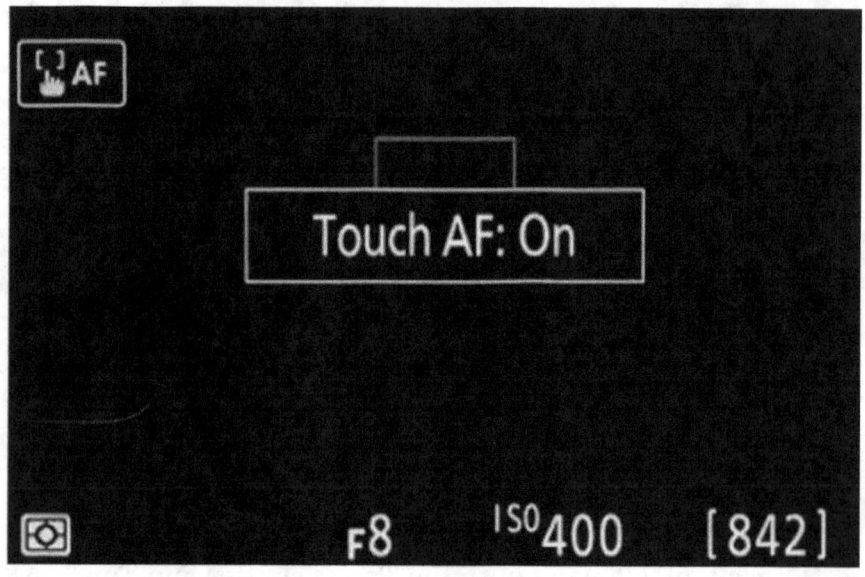

the monitor to start focusing.

5. A popup window titled "Touch shutter/AF: Off" will show when you touch the Touch shutter/AF icon one last time.

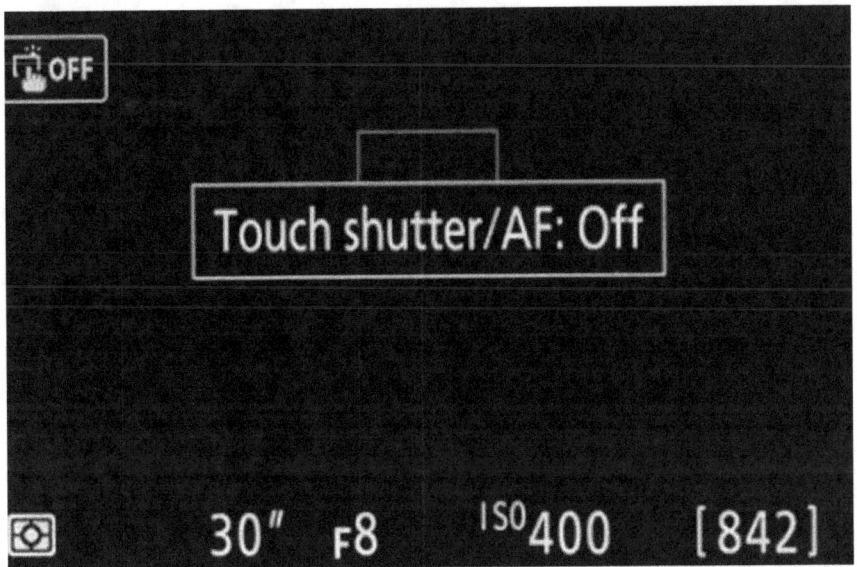

The camera will not react to screen touches by auto focusing or releasing the shutter when you see the OFF word in the touch icon.

Note: This feature (tap shooting) comes in handy when you wish to activate the shutter with little shaking.

UTILIZING THE Z7 WITH EXTERNAL ELECTRONIC FLASH UNIT

One advantage of the Z7 is that it can be used with a wide range of both vintage and modern Nikon Speedlight electronic flash units that use the Creative Lighting System (CLS). However, it is crucial to comprehend the Nikon Creative Lighting System (CLS) before delving into an analysis of any Z7-compatible electronic flash. The following are the characteristics of the CLS:

1. Intelligent through-the-lens exposure control, or i-TTL: This feature uses the same RGB exposure sensor that is used for continuous light readings to compute exposure based on a monitor pre-flash that is fired just before the main burst. As a result of the system's intelligence, you can make intricate modifications like, matching the flash exposure with the ambient light exposure when you take pictures in the daytime to enhance the shadows.

2. Advanced wireless lighting: This feature which can be called AWL for short, is a system that communicates triggering and exposure information to external flash units that are situated within an acceptable distance (about thirty feet) but are not physically attached to the camera. It does this by using the same pre-flash principle. To prevent your flash units from being activated by the master flash of another Nikon photographer nearby, you will be able to partition multiple flash units into up to three distinct "groups"

and communicate with them via any one of four "channels."

3. Flash value locking (FV Lock): This kind of technology lets you lock in the current flash exposure. This way, you can measure the flash exposure of a subject that is not in the center of the frame, reframe, and use that value for more exposures. To carry out this task, you can define the Fn button. When the flash is attached in the hot shoe and FV lock is engaged, the Z7 only measures the 8mm center region, even if Matrix metering is used.

4. Auto FP High-Speed Sync: When utilizing shutter speeds higher than 1/200th of a second, focal plane HS sync enables external flash synchronization. Shutter rates up to 1/8,000th second can be used with a suitable flash with a camera such as the Z7, although the flash's light is only partially used, and its range is limited.

5. Focus assist: The Z7 is equipped with focus assist lighting, but the CLS system also makes it possible to integrate the wide-area AF-assist illuminator onto a flash connection cable or the front of the flash unit itself. Auxiliary focus aid lighting provides coverage that is either further away or broader.

6. Zoom Coverage: Some CLS-compatible flash units come with a powered zoom head that can be used to adjust the flash's coverage area to match the focal length of the lens

that is being used, as determined by the camera and sent to the flash. It allows one to manually zoom as well.

7. Flash color information communication: Depending on how long the flash burst lasts, a CLS-compatible flash's precise color temperature may change. As the burst proceeds, the flash's hue changes from being somewhat blue to redder. In order to modify white balance in AWB mode based on the real color information of the flash exposure, the Speedlight will be able to transmit information to the camera.

Additionally, Nikon provides a large selection of CLS-compatible external flash units, ranging from the high-end SB-5000 to the budget-friendly SB-300.

Nikon SB-300

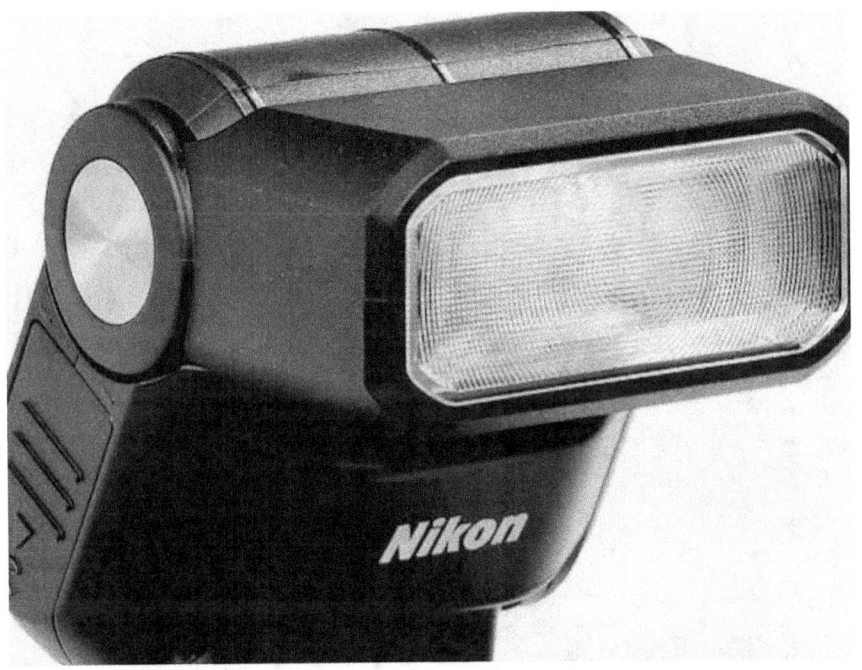

This entry-level Speedlight is the smallest and most basic model in the Nikon Speedlight lineup. The SB-300's feature set is simple and constrained, making it ideal for point-and-shoot photography as well as a few somewhat more sophisticated methods. At ISO 100, the SB-300 has a reasonable guide number of 18/59. Therefore, its primary benefit is to raise the flash slightly above the camera to increase coverage and reduce the possibility of red-eye symptoms. When pointing straight ahead, the flash head tilts up to 120 degrees, with click stops at 90, 75, 60, and 120 degrees. This device possesses a zoomed in flash head. The SB-300 requires two AAA batteries and weighs 3.4 ounces less than the SB-400 it replaces.

Nikon SB-500

With two AA batteries, this Nikon flash unit can operate for up to 140 flashes and has a reference number of 24/79 at ISO 100. It also recycles quickly, taking just roughly 3.5 seconds. At its strongest setting, it can be used as fill light for still photography. It also has an integrated LED video light with three output levels.

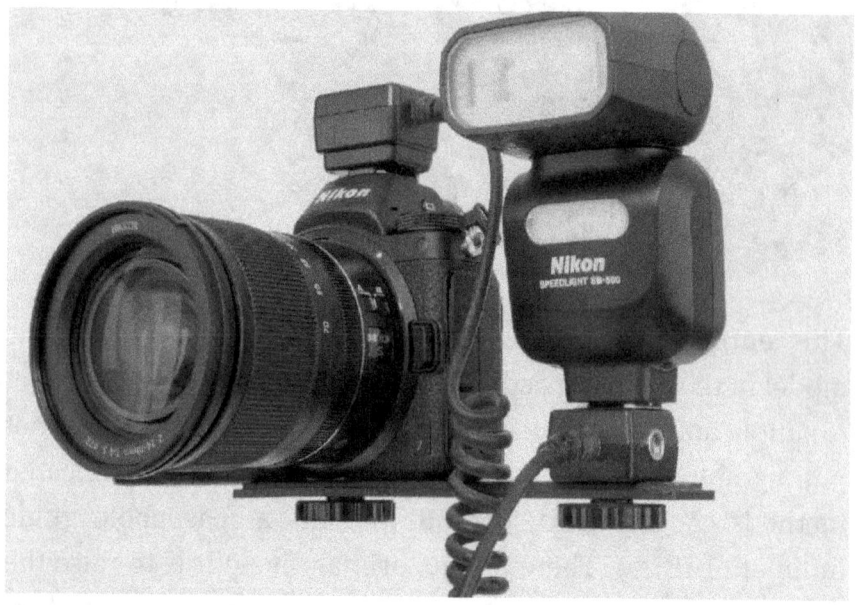

With click-stops at 0, 60, 75, and 90 degrees, the SB-500's head can tilt up to ninety degrees. Its 180-degree horizontal rotation allows for versatile bounce-flash illumination in both left and right directions. Despite its short zoom range, the SB-700 is still a superior choice if you require a zoom head to change the flash's output to properly disperse light at different focal lengths.

Nikon SB-700

When set to the 35mm zoom setting, this device offers a guide number of 28/92 (meters/feet) at ISO 100. Numerous characteristics of the top-model SB-910 are included in it, such as 14mm with an integrated diffuser panel and zoomable flash coverage equivalent to the field of view of a 16-56mm lens on the Z7 (or 24-120mm settings with a full-frame camera). It offers a wireless Commander mode and an integrated modeling flash capability.

However, the SB-5000 and SB-910 have a few key functions that the SB-700 does not. These distinctions may or may not matter to you, depending on how you use your Speedlight. Among them are:

1. Not Repeating Flash Mode: The SB-7000 is not capable of producing captivating stroboscopic effects, unlike the SB-5000 or the previous SB-910/900 models.

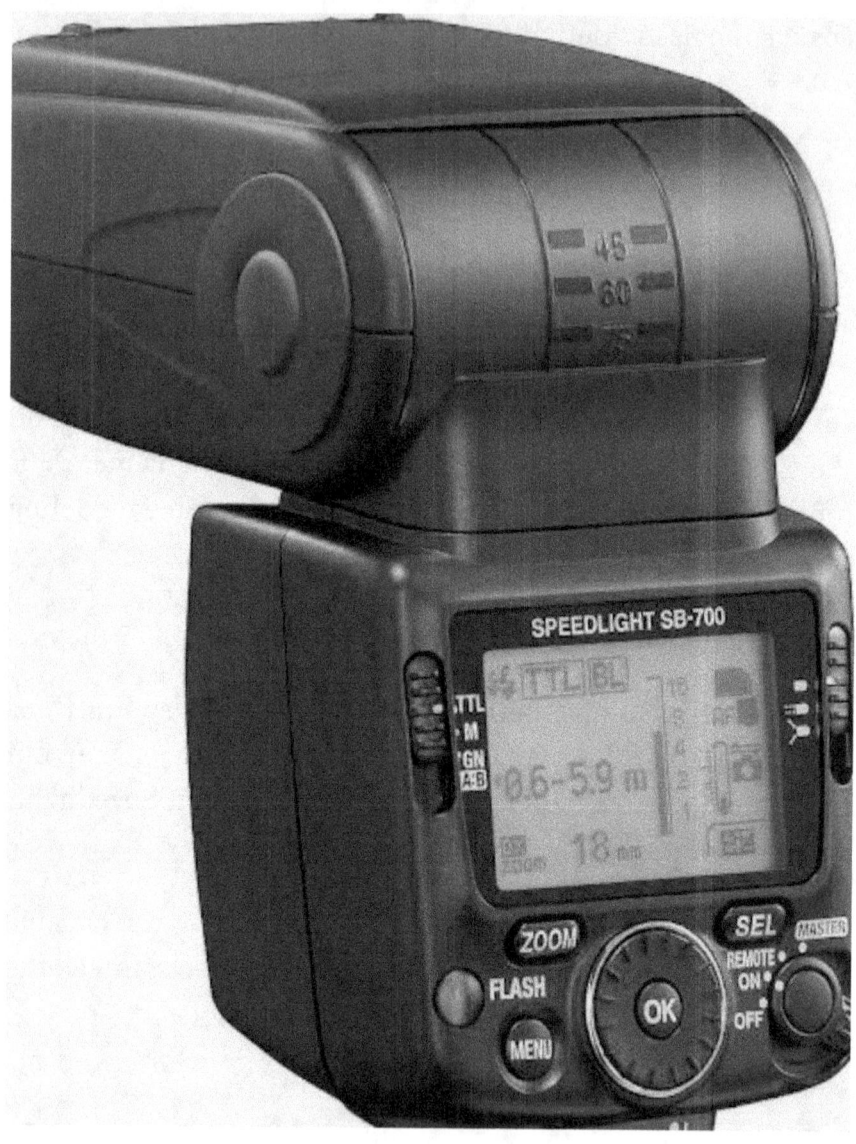

2. Restricted zoom range: The zoom head of the SB-700 is restricted to 24-120mm, and it can extend to 14mm with the diffuser panel. Adjusting the zoom head to the focal length optimally aligns the flash coverage with the field

of view, preventing unnecessary illumination outside the frame.

The Nikon SB-R200

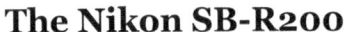

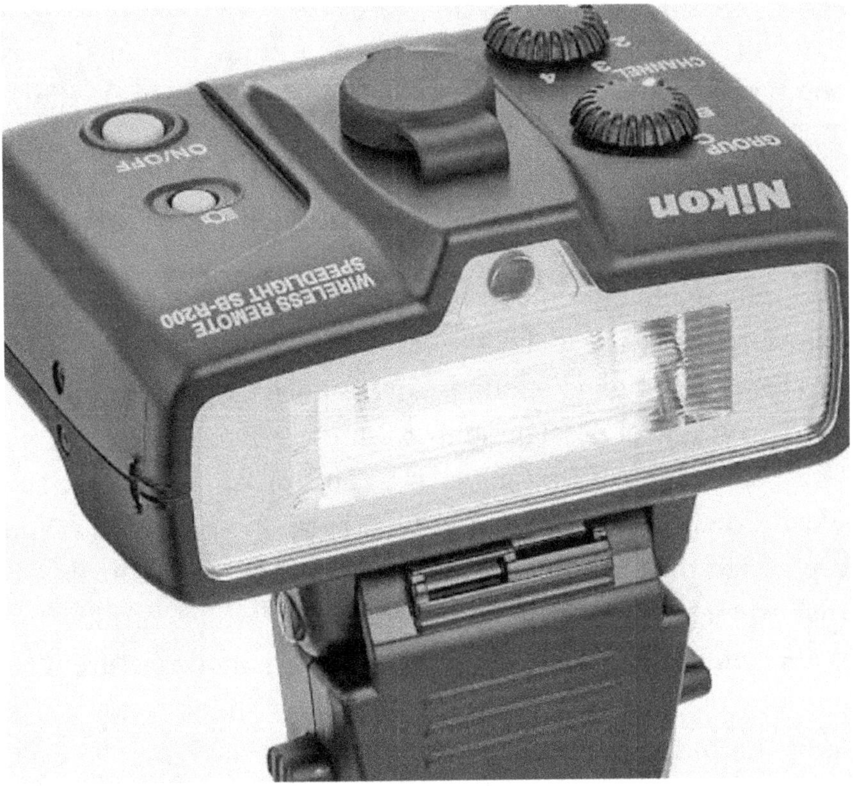

Often bought in pairs for use with the Nikon R1 and R1C1 Wireless Close-Up Speedlight systems, this specialized wireless-only flash is very helpful for close-up photography. As one would anticipate for a device intended to take pictures of objects that are often inches from the camera, its output power is minimal at 10/33 (meters/feet) at ISO 100. The flash head moves downwards to 60 degrees and up to 45 degrees (with detents every 15 degrees in both directions), but its coverage angle is set at 78 degrees horizontally and 60 degrees vertically. Here, "up" and "down" have a distinct meaning since the two flash units are on the sides and titled either toward or away from the optical axis when the SB-R200 is placed on the SX-1 Attachment Ring that is positioned around the lens. It is compatible with manual, D-TTL, TTL (film cameras), and i-TTL modes.

Making Use of Flash Exposure Compensation

You can manually add or remove exposure from the flash exposure determined by the Z7 if the exposure your flash produces is not good enough. You can use Custom Setting f2: Custom Control Assignment to attach Flash Mode/Flash Compensation to a button, such as Fn1, or you can utilize the Flash Compensation option in the Photo Shooting menu. You can assign the flash mode option to a button in the camera, so that when you press the assigned button whilst turning the main command dial, it will activate the flash mode feature. You can also activate Flash Compensation by holding down the assigned button simultaneously with the sub-command dial. Note; you can make modifications in 1/3 EV increments by changing from −3 EV to +1 EV.

Similar to standard exposure compensation, you can not undo a change unless you click the Flash button and turn the sub-command dial, until the monochrome control panel and viewfinder display 0; this process resets the adjustment you made. Press the Flash button to check the current flash

148

exposure compensation setting. Note; both the control panel and the viewfinder will display an icon when you are utilizing compensation.

Alternatively, you can use Custom Setting e3: Exposure Compensation for Flash to just account for the backdrop or to balance flash exposure and ambient light over the full frame. This feature controls how exposure compensation affects the flash level on the camera. If flash is being used, you have the option to change either one or both. When employing flash in addition to exposure compensation, this option solely impacts ambient exposure compensation. It also establishes the method for applying ambient exposure adjustment in situations when a flash unit is also going to provide some light. The application of the exposure compensation ambient has been explained below:

1. Entire frame: Ambient and flash exposure compensation are adjusted for the full frame when you apply ambient exposure compensation, which is done by rotating the main command dial and pushing the EV button on top of the camera to the right of the ISO button. This equalizes the two components' exposure.

2. Background only: Only ambient exposure compensation is altered when this option is used; flash exposure compensation is left unchanged. As a result, exposure compensation is only used in your image's backdrop, which is usually lit by ambient light. Lastly, compensation for flash exposure remains unaffected.

www.ingramcontent.com/pod-product-compliance
Lightning Source LLC
Chambersburg PA
CBHW071045290526
45795CB00004B/1330